Management
by
Initiatives

A New Paradigm *for*
Executing Business Strategy *and*
Achieving Meaningful Business Results

TAB EDWARDS

MANAGEMENT
by
INITIATIVES

A New Paradigm *for*
Executing Business Strategy *and*
Achieving Meaningful Business Results

!
TMBE

TMBE, PHILADELPHIA, PENNSYLVANIA 19129

TMBE / *The Water Group*

Printed in the United States of America. Except as permitted under the United States Copyright Act of 1976, no part of this publication may be reproduced or distributed in any form or by any means, or stored in a data base or retrieval system, without the prior written permission of the publisher.

ISBN 978-0-9909866-3-8

This publication is designed to provide authoritative information in regards to the subject matter covered. It is sold with the understanding that the publisher is not engaged in rendering legal, accounting, or other professional services. If legal advice or other expert assistance is required, the services of a competent professional person should be sought.

—From a declaration of principles jointly adopted by a committee of the American Bar Association and a committee of publishers.

Tab Edwards books are available at special quantity discounts to use as premiums and promotions, or for use in corporate training programs. For more information, please visit the website TabEdwards.com.

Designed by Water Creative
Philadelphia, PA.

1   3   5   7   9   10   8   6   4   2

TTX

CONTENTS

• • •

THE BUG BUFFET

· · ·

QUESTION:

Why did the chicken cross the road?

The answer to this age-old riddle is not as simple as you were previously led to believe. Of course, the traditional answer to this riddle—and, undoubtedly, the answer you were thinking of—is "to get to the other side." But, is that the real reason the chicken crossed the road?

The riddle is first thought to have appeared in print in an 1847 issue of *The Knickerbocker* (*New-York Monthly Magazine*), a New York City literary magazine founded in 1833. It appeared as below:

"...There are 'quips and quillets'
which *seem* actual conundrums, but yet are
none. Of such is this: 'Why does a chicken
cross the street?' Are you 'out of town?'
Do you 'give it up?' Well, then: 'Because it
wants to get on the other side!'

Over time, this "quip" or "quillet" took many different forms, ultimately becoming the riddle we know today—changing from *Why does a chicken cross the street?*
to *Why did the chicken cross the road?* Even as it is told
today, many people believe the riddle is not simply as
it appears—a harmless conundrum—but that instead
there is a deeper meaning or message within the riddle.
For instance, some philosophers interpret "the road"
as a path to somewhere, a pathway to "the other side"
rather than an actual *street* (the original word used in
the riddle), as we think of a paved or dirt road traveled by cars. Some hypothesize that the chicken wants
to get to the "other side," to the afterlife or the next life.
Some have even gone so far as to conjecture that the
chicken knows that "roads" are traveled by cars and that
the chicken is on a suicide mission to get to the afterlife!
Completely serious—no kidding.

Such a proposition, of course, would rest on the assumption that chickens have consciousness and sen-
tience. At the 2012 Francis Crick Memorial Conference, focused on "Consciousness in Humans and Non-
Human Animals," a prominent international group of

scientists reached agreement that humans are not the only conscious beings; other animals, specifically mammals and birds, are indeed conscious. In a paper entitled *The Cambridge Declaration on Consciousness in Non-Human Animals*, they wrote that "Convergent evidence indicates that non-human animals have the neuroanatomical, neurochemical, and neurophysiological substrates of conscious states along with the capacity to exhibit intentional behaviors."

Based on these findings and others which show that chickens actually display empathy, it would seem that the chicken wanting to cross the road in fact had consciousness, although the group of scientists didn't attempt to define what consciousness actually is. The truth is, defining consciousness is very complex and, frankly, no one really knows how to do so. And even if we assumed that the chicken was a conscious being with the ability to feel emotions, it is still not known whether the chicken had the ability to reason. In other words, as it relates to the chicken wanting to commit suicide, did the chicken know that by walking into traffic and getting run over by a car it would be committing suicide as a means—in the mind of the chicken—to get to the afterlife, the "other side?" I have my doubts.

Even without getting overly philosophical, there is enough evidence to suggest that the "quip" or "quillet" about the chicken was simply a riddle that falls into the *anti-humor* category. Anti-humor is a type of riddle where the joke's set-up leads the listener to expect a challenging punchline, but the answer is, instead, a simple, obvious, "duh" statement of fact. Why did the chicken cross the road? Why would *anyone* cross the road? To get to the other side. Duh.

Supporting evidence for the proverbial chicken question as simply a riddle, joke, or witticism can be found in William Shakespeare's *Othello*. In the play, Shakespeare created the Clown, whose brief appearance, in a discussion with Cassio, seems to be for no other reason than to illustrate that words can be untrustworthy and can have different meanings in different contexts:

Cassio: Dost thou hear, mine honest friend?

Clown: No, I hear not your honest friend. I hear *you.*

Cassio: Prithee, keep up thy quillets.

What's important to note about this brief dialogue are: (1) the Clown used *anti-humor* when responding to Cassio ("No, I hear not *your honest friend.* I hear *you*"), and (2) Cassio referred to the Clown's reply as "quillets." The word "quillet" is not used now, but when *Othello* was written in 1603 and when the chicken piece was published in *The Knickerbocker* in 1847 it was still used, and it meant quibbles, puns, or a deliberate misreading from the obvious. Given this understanding of the words "quip" and "quillet" as used in the original form of the riddle, and given the author's answer to the two posed questions, it becomes clear that the questions "Why does a chicken cross the street?" and "Are you 'out of town?'" (think about *that* one) are simply riddles in the form of anti-humor: "Well, then: 'Because it wants to get on the other side!'"

Which brings us back to the original question: *Why does a chicken cross the street* or *why did the chicken cross the road*? Phrased differently, what was the reason for the chicken to cross the street? What was its purpose?

Maybe the chicken knew about planning and there was a reason, an ultimate purpose, for crossing the road—other than to simply get to the other side of the street. Is this implausible? Not in the least. Research from the University of Bristol has proven that chickens are very smart. In multiple cognitive and behavioral sophistication tests, chickens outperformed not just dogs and cats, but four-year-old human children. So, since we know that dogs, cats, and children can make plans and execute them for an ultimate purpose, why can't a chicken?

So I ask the question again: Why *did* the chicken cross the road?

An examination of the rationale for the chicken crossing the road must begin with the assumption that the chicken had a plan that required it to cross the road. It must also begin with the question: Why *would* a chicken cross the road in the first place?

Most chickens have been domesticated and live on farms, but wild chickens can still be found in India, Southeast Asia, and Hawaii, among other places. For this discussion, I will focus on the *wild chicken,* since the wild chicken is most likely to be found crossing streets and roads. Specifically, I will refer to the wild chickens on the Hawaiian Island of Kauai, where the population is so large that locals joke that the "official" birds of the island are wild chickens.

Wild chickens eat bugs, *lots* of bugs, and bugs can be found in abundance in parks, gardens, and the natural foliage found throughout the island. Kauai, in fact, is called *the garden isle* for its lush vegetation. A major "road" running through Kauai is the 56/560 Kuhio Highway which, for much of its route, is framed on one or both sides by bug-populated vegetation. The highway is heavily crossed by wild chickens, as evidenced by what locals call *roadkill roosters*: all the wild chickens that have tried to cross the road and haven't made it. These birds were apparently crossing the road to get to what has been referred to as a "bug buffet" on the other side of the highway. This gives us some insight into why the wild chickens cross the road: to eat. And why do people and animals eat? According to psychologist Abraham Maslow, the reason we eat is to satisfy the basic physiological need of hunger. Eating and drinking are necessary for survival.

So, it turns out, the wild chickens crossed the road, not to simply get to the other side, but to eat the food necessary for satiation and ultimately survival. This is their ultimate reason for crossing the road, their purpose, their goal.

A standard-sized chicken will eat approximately one-quarter pound of food daily; this is the quantitative measure of food necessary for the chicken to achieve satiation, to feel "full" throughout the day. When the chicken eats enough bugs and other food to the point of being full or satisfied, it can rest assured that it has achieved its food requirement and that—but for the inability to dodge oncoming traffic—it will continue to live.

The wild chicken that crossed the road had a clear plan: to eat to satisfy its hunger. To execute its plan, it had to get to the "bug buffet" and eat enough bugs to fill its stomach. And the way to the bug buffet is to cross the road. Looking at the chicken as a strategist, we find that the chicken that was successful at getting to the bugs alive had successfully developed and executed its strategy.

A breakdown of the chicken's plan reveals a crude-yet-successful strategy consisting of all major strategic elements: goal, objective, initiative, and tasks.

- *The plan*: A plan is a strategy, which is an approach for achieving some desired outcome; the purpose, the *goal*;

- *The goal*: In the chicken's case, its goal was to eat and fill its belly with bugs and satisfy its hunger, staving off starvation;

- *The objective*: To achieve its goal of filling its belly with bugs and satisfying its hunger, the chicken would have to eat approximately one-quarter pound of bugs in the course of a day;

- *The initiative*: To fill its belly with bugs, the chicken would have to get to the food source, and the bug buffet (the food source) is located on the other side of the road. Therefore, *the chicken must cross the road*. This is why the chicken did it: to eat, *not* to simply get to the other side.

In the case of the wild chicken, the most important strategic element was the **initiative**: *getting to the other side of the road alive* so that it could eat bugs, satisfy its hunger, and stay alive. Establishing the goal is necessary, because it establishes what the chicken strives to accomplish. But, setting the goal *does not* lead to a full stomach; it is not actionable in and of itself.

Defining an objective (to eat its daily one-quarter pound requirement of bugs) is necessary because it establishes a measurable target that will tell the chicken whether or not it has successfully met its daily food requirement; whether or not it has satisfied its goal. Defining the objective is necessary, but, like the goal, it is not itself actionable.

Defining the initiative to cross the road to get to the bugs, the food source, is necessary because it provides the actionable step necessary to achieve the objective (eat one-quarter-pound of bugs) and, consequently, accomplish the goal (satisfy hunger). The initiative is the element of the strategy where the chicken engages itself in a Q&A session:

Q: What must I do to eat the bugs?

A: *Get to the bug buffet.*

Q: How do I get to the bug buffet?

A: *Cross the road without getting killed.*

And, having seen the fate of his fellow chickens that did not make it across, the chicken might execute the task of *flying* across the road (since wild chickens can fly).

Unlike the goal and objective, the initiative *is actionable*. It is the first stage of a strategic plan where the chicken's desires (goals and objectives) are made real. It is the element of the strategy that the chicken must successfully execute; otherwise it will not be able to eat the quarter pound of bugs and, will eventually, die of starvation. Initiative execution is, therefore, critical to the survival of the chicken, just like the successful accomplishment of an organization's goals is critical to its survival in the public or private sector.

An organization's goals—just like the chicken's—cannot be accomplished if the initiatives that define how the goals and objectives will be accomplished are not executed successfully. It is my contention that strategy initiatives are the most critical layer of a strategic plan because, if the initiatives are not properly defined and successfully executed, the organization's strategy will in all likelihood fail.

Imagine if the chicken could *not* cross the road …

ONE

THE PURPOSE OF STRATEGY

• • •

Strategy has been described as *the process by which purpose is translated into action.* I am a fan of this succinct definition because, though brief, it embodies the central tenets that I believe define a strategy: the purpose of an entity dictates its desired results, which are realized by a plan of action.

Many definitions of strategy exist, including: "purposeful action"; a "design for action"; "a plan to achieve stratagems"; "something you do to make the organization better"; as well as other definitions in between. While the definition of strategy can vary depending on whose opinion you rely on, ultimately, I believe that strategy is about two things: *survival* and *prosperity.*

In a competitive landscape—an environment defined by organizations targeting buyers with competing, viable offerings; buyers with better information, higher expectations, and more choices; changing demographics affecting the market opportunity; and global expansion giving rise to new competitors and complex regulations—strategy is about survival, enduring through adversity caused by the competitive landscape.

Strategy is also about prosperity: remaining viable, achieving "success" as defined by that which the strategy is developed to achieve, and thriving.

The idea of strategy as a means to survival and prosperity can be seen as far back as 1925 when the American biophysicist Alfred Lotka and Italian mathematician Vito Volterra developed a model of interactions between two species competing for limiting resources, and, more recently, in 1934 by Georgyi Frantsevitch (G.F.) Gause who developed the competitive exclusion principle, sometimes referred to as *Gause's Law of Competitive Exclusion* or more simply as *Gause's Law.* He demonstrated experimentally that two species that compete for the same resources in one homogeneous habitat cannot stably coexist.

Using two closely-related Paramecium species to create competition for an energy source (a desirable resource), Gause demonstrated that the two protozoan would fight for the resource until one protozoan successfully won it. According to Gause, "Owing to its advantages, ... one of the species in a mixed population drives out the other entirely."

As demonstrated by Gause more than 80 years ago, the notion that the competitor which possessed some advantage would capture the market and drive out its competition, resonates with strategic thinking today; managers understand that to beat the competition and survive or thrive, an organization must develop a sustainable competitive advantage, whether at the corporate or business-unit level.

BUSINESS-UNIT-LEVEL STRATEGY

Although the ideas and practices offered throughout this book have applicability across all strategy levels, the book's primary focus will be on strategies developed at the business-unit level. While there is significant overlap between the two types of strategies—the business-unit-level strategy should support, align, and integrate with general corporate strategy—there are distinctions.

Corporate strategy is about exploiting the benefits of the industry in which the Company operates, its organizational structure, and its resources to create *value* for its stakeholders. Business-unit-level strategy is focused on creating a sustainable *competitive advantage* within a market subset of the industry in which the organization conducts business; it defines how the organization will compete.

In 1965, the scientist and business manager H. Igor Ansoff—called "the father of modern strategic thinking"—published a book entitled *Corporate Strategy*, the first book to concentrate solely on this subject and has been referred to as the most elaborate strategic planning model in the literature. The "elaborate" nature of the book's processes and checklists proved too detailed for many readers, and Ansoff himself eventually recognized that it too often resulted in "paralysis by analysis."

In the 1970s, Ansoff approached the field of study by introducing flexibility into the strategic planning process, and considered management decision-making from three perspectives: strategic; administrative; and operational, and along the way, acknowledged that there was a gap between high-level strategies and execution, and that corporate strategies should contain an organizational action process. In his book *Strategic Management*, he wrote:

> The major aim [of this book] is to bridge the gap between theory and practice by providing an explanatory theory which can be helpful both for the evaluation and for the development of practical technology. In the natural sciences such explanations go under the name of *applied theory*—an intermediate level of knowledge between pure theory and engineering. Applied theory deals with generic concepts, but in a format and language which is translatable into practical problem-solving.

As it related to corporate strategy being translatable into practical problem-solving (an action plan), he wrote that this translation is essential if a connection to practical applications is to be made visible. In other words, corporate strategies should be made actionable if they are to have value. Ansoff, thus, distinguished between *strategic planning* and *strategic management*.

Strategic planning, he wrote, is focused on optimal strategy decisions, whereas strategic management is focused on producing strategic results; strategic planning is an analytical process, whereas strategic management is an organizational action process. Therefore, strategic planning is about choosing things to do, and strategic management is about choosing things to do, the people who will do them, and then getting it done. Strategic management recognizes the role played by the individual and incorporates strategic thinking into management throughout all organizational units.

The strategic management concept was an early articulation of business-unit-level strategy. A core idea of this line of thinking was that organizations must adopt a unified approach to the activities in which they engage rather than allowing each business unit to pursue its own, separate plans. A strategy is a vehicle for aligning all of an organization's plans toward the fulfillment of a unified, common goal, driving alignment between all of an organization's business units and functional areas, and eliminating inconsistencies and wastes of effort & resources. This gave rise to the concept of *business-unit-level strategy*.

A common feature of effective organizations is that they are structured into discrete sub-units, each with their own decision-making autonomy, which allows business unit managers who have relevant knowledge and are, therefore, best suited to make decisions related to the business unit for which they have managerial responsibility to make decisions. It stands to reason that these business units must be empowered with the ability to drive their own business-unit level strategies that are aligned with and in support of the organization's overarching corporate strategy.

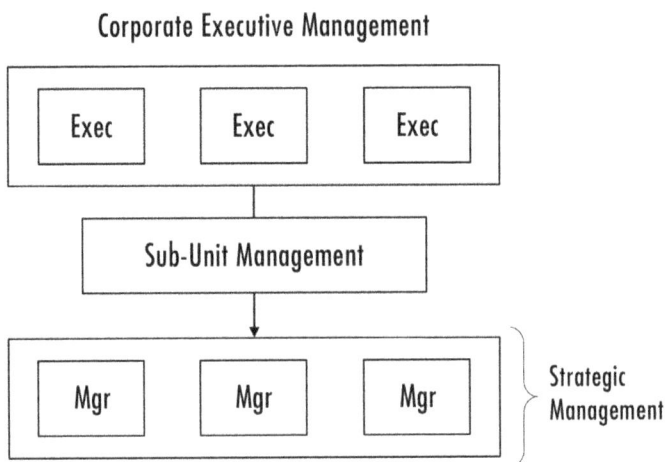

Corporate Executive Management

| Exec | Exec | Exec |

Sub-Unit Management

| Mgr | Mgr | Mgr | Strategic Management

This raises the interesting question: What exactly do managers do, anyway?

THE ROLE OF THE MANAGER

As hard as this may be to believe, genuine uncertainty remains about what managers do for their organizations. A primary reason is that each organizational structure implies (and, in a sense, dictates) a specific function and various responsibilities for its management.

Organizations cannot make decisions, people are an organization's decision-making element; an organization does not exist outside of its people. The activities in which an organization engages are determined by people—traditionally, some form of a *manager*. Managers serve a special function within organizations and have decision-making and execution responsibilities.

So what is a manager? Simplistically, a manager can be described as a person with the authority to decide on key issues while considering the structure, function, and "needs" of the market in which the organization does business. Managers develop and manage people (they are ultimately held responsible for their subordinates' decisions and activities), build coalitions, allocate resources, and decide upon go-forward actions. At the same time, the manager is a figurehead, representative, information disseminator, and networker. To quote Henry Mintzberg, a well-known management scholar and author of the 1973 book *The Nature of Managerial Work*, "Managing is about helping organizations and units to get things done, which means action."

I am in absolute agreement that managers' primary focus should be on accomplishment, which I define as the achievement of business-unit and organizational objectives (which are manifest in strategy initiatives).

To accomplish something means to bring it to its *goal*, to achieve a defined and necessary end. Isn't this what managers are ultimately hired to do? Managers should always be mindful of their purpose within the organization and focus on achieving the goals and objectives—the necessary *ends*—they are charged with rather than simply engaging in unrelated activities and day-to-day busy work. Without guidance, individuals will do the things they *think* are important, often resulting in uncoordinated, divergent, even conflicting decisions and actions. Any activity in which a manager engages that does not directly support organizational goals is a wasted effort.

MANAGEMENT BY OBJECTIVES (MBO)

The concept of Management by Objectives (MBO)— and their use as they relate to general business management—was proposed by Peter Drucker in his seminal 1954 management book *The Practice of Management.* Though Drucker is credited with creating "management by objectives," previous management thinkers, such as Ralph C. Davis wrote about the need for objectives as a foundation of management in 1937. Davis, however, never used the term MBO; Drucker was the first to publish the concept and to use the term in his publication, where he argued:

"Setting objectives enables a business to get where it should be going rather than be the plaything of weather, winds and accidents. A business must be managed by setting objectives for it. To manage a business means, therefore, to manage by objectives."

He also made the case that "Objectives are needed in every area where performance and results directly and vitally affect the survival and prosperity of the business." MBO is a concept wherein the performance of each employee in an organization—not simply managers—is measured against defined objectives; objectives that support business goals. The idea is that aligning goals and their subordinate objectives throughout the organization will improve organizational performance. This is consistent with the proposal that I will share throughout this book that all managers in an organization (and, as appropriate, non-managers, too) should participate in the strategic planning process to improve plan execution.

Drucker's Management by Objectives principles that are consistent with my ideas on management and organizational effectiveness are:

- Cascading of organizational goals and objectives;
- Specific objectives for each member;
- Participative decision-making; and
- Explicit time period.

While Drucker's MBO conceptualization sits at the forefront of the management proposition, the most compelling definition of management by objectives that I have read is provided by former University of Massachusetts business school professor George S. Odiorne (who, incidentally, wrote a book entitled *Management Decisions by Objectives* (1965)) where he argued:

> The system of management by objectives can be described as a process whereby the superior and subordinate managers of an organization jointly identify its common goals, define each individual's major area of responsibility in terms of the results expected of him, and use these measures as guides for operating the unit and assessing the contribution of each of its members.

The bottom line is this: managers should be charged with and measured by their success in achieving business objectives and thereby supporting the accomplishment of organizational goals within a strategic framework.

THE ELEMENTS OF A STRATEGY

• • •

STRATEGIC PLANNING VS. STRATEGIC PLAN VS. STRATEGY

In Chapter 1, I made a distinction between strategic planning and strategic management, and before proceeding, it is important to distinguish strategic planning, a strategic plan, and a strategy to eliminate confusion moving forward.

Strategy is the process which translates purpose into action. *Strategic planning* is the process organizations follow to set the direction for the organization, allocate its resources to support that direction, define how it's going to get there, and determine how it will know whether or not it got there within the desired timeframe. In other words, it is the process of creating a *strategy*.

The strategic planning process can be carried out in various ways depending on the size of the organization, its structure, the industry in which it operates, geography, its available resources, its competitors, its profit status (e.g., for-profit, non-profit, not-for-profit), and other factors. But, ultimately, each type of entity engages in the strategic planning process to develop a go-forward plan.

It is worth noting that many strategy thought-leaders assert that strategic planning (especially long-range strategic planning) has become outdated over the years because of the pace at which change occurs in the world today (as compared with the rate of change when strategic planning began to emerge). Academic and author Henry Mintzberg wrote that, because organizations must deal with uncertainty, it is therefore dangerous to articulate a strategy. He went so far as to say that, "Setting oneself on a predetermined course in unknown waters is the perfect way to sail straight into an iceberg." In recent years, however, it has been shown that strategic planning positively affects organizational performance, and that some researchers who have concluded the contrary appear to have been incorrect.

A *strategic plan* is an explicitly-stated documentation of a strategy. In that sense, a strategy and a strategic plan are synonymous. During the strategy development (strategic planning) process, organizations will customarily follow a model to aid effective plan development. Over the years, there have been many strategy development and strategic planning models created to guide organizations as they engage in the process, including models with names, such as: the Bryson Model, Issues-Based Planning Model, Alignment Model, the Water Method, Scenario Planning Model, "Organic" (or Self-Organizing) Planning Model, and the Real-Time Planning Model, to name just a few. Whatever the model, they all contain various elements to drive standardization, consistency, and alignment between the elements. I will describe these elements that will be found in the vast majority of business-unit level strategies that have been developed.

It is worth noting that there is a difference between the aims of corporate strategies and business-unit strategies, and the desired outcomes of each will dictate elements of the respective strategies.

The purpose of corporate-level strategy is value creation through the market activities in which the organization engages and how it allocates resources to gain a competitive advantage. Renowned economist and researcher Michael Porter identified two corporate strategy models: portfolio management and restructuring, where the organization fundamentally changes underperforming companies to extract value from them. Other management educators have proposed additional models. While there is no one model for developing corporate strategy, common elements include some combination of: organizational resource allocation; the businesses in which the organization engages; and the organization's structure.

The purpose of business-unit-level strategy is to gain a competitive advantage. Porter identified two types of competitive advantage: low cost and differentiation, meaning the ability to provide "unique and superior value" leading to a competitive advantage. Just as with corporate-level strategies, there is no one standard format, framework, or model for creating business-unit-level strategies. Generally, however, I have found that there are common elements that comprise most business-unit-level strategies, including: goals, objectives, and action plans—which are described in greater detail in subsequent paragraphs.

The relationship between the corporate-level and business-unit-level strategies can be seen in the link between the corporate-level strategy's pursuit of value creation and its use of the created value to generate a competitive advantage at the business-unit level, and vice-versa.

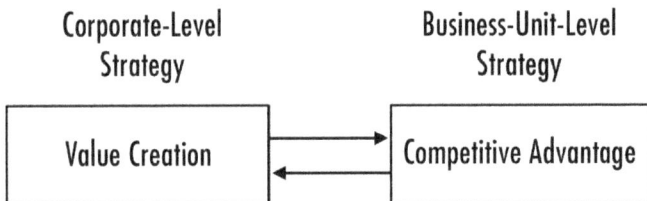

Corporate-Level Strategy	Business-Unit-Level Strategy
Value Creation	⟶ ⟵ Competitive Advantage

The hierarchy and relationship between the strategy types—corporate-level and business-unit level—are represented in the diagram below.

Strategic Hierarchy

Corporate-Level Strategy

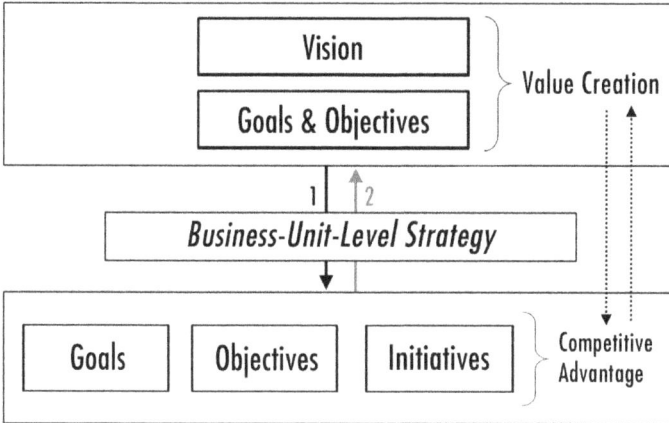

Vision
Goals & Objectives

} Value Creation

1 ↑2

Business-Unit-Level Strategy

Goals	Objectives	Initiatives

} Competitive Advantage

BASIC ELEMENTS OF A BUSINESS-UNIT-LEVEL STRATEGY

As discussed, a strategy fundamentally expresses an organization's desired future state and the as-of-today requirements to get there.

An organization will define a long-term vision of what it wants to be or become in some future, multi-year timeframe. To fulfill this vision, the organization must develop a plan for how it will get there, a plan consisting of shorter-term targets and milestones referred to as goals and objectives, and a supporting action plan to achieve said goals and objectives.

Goals

A goal is a broad, often-qualitative intended outcome of an initiative or an activity in which the company is engaged that indicates success or improvement in organizational performance or a reinforcement of the organization's values; they are the outcomes an organization must achieve if it is to effectively work toward its mission and achieve its vision. Goals take the form of "To [Action Verb] [Noun]" and are not always achievable in the desired short-to-medium-term timeframe. For example, a market development goal could be "To become the #2 software provider in the Northeast Region of United States (in dollar sales)."

Objectives

An objective is the measurable (usually quantitative) manifestation of the goal which it supports. In other words, the objective defines in measurable/quantitative (and time-specific) terms how the company will know that it has accomplished the goal which the objective supports. For example, if a goal is "To become the #2 software provider in the Northeast Region of the United States (in dollar sales)" and, last year, the #2 software provider sold $X in software, then the objective supporting the goal would be defined in such a way that, if the objective is achieved, the company would know it had accomplished its goal. For example, a supporting objective could be: "Achieve $X + $1 in software sales by December 31st."

Initiatives

Once the goal(s) and objective(s) are defined, specific "initiatives" must be articulated to support the objectives. An initiative is a project or other undertaking that defines what must be done to achieve the objective it supports. So, if the objective is to "Achieve $X + $1 in software sales by December 31st," the associated initiative(s) must define the project(s) that will lead to $X + $1 million in sales by December 31st.

Tasks and Action Items

Once the Initiatives are defined, a set of tasks or action items must be developed which define the specific activities that must be executed to realize the initiative it supports. Each task or action item must define the person who is accountable for task completion and has ultimate ownership for it, and the person who is responsible for executing the task (i.e., does the work) if that person is different from the person who is accountable for task completion. Furthermore, the resources (human resources, money, and tools, etc.) that will be needed to complete a task must be identified.

Action Plan

The action plan makes the strategy "real" and tangible for an organization's personnel. It translates an organization's vision and mission into tangible objectives, measures, and executable actions. Many people mistakenly believe that a strategy's action plan is the collective set of tasks to be performed to realize the associated initiative; that is incorrect. The action plan portion of a strategy includes all elements that make the goal real, including the quantitative/measurable objectives, the related initiatives, and the associated tasks. This relationship is illustrated in the diagram below.

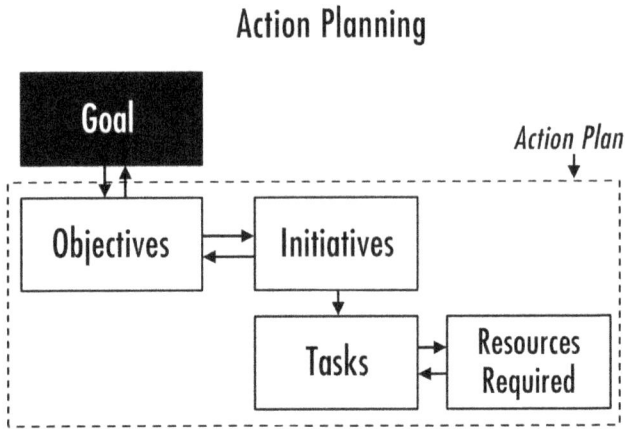

Action Planning

```
┌─────────────┐
│    Goal     │                          Action Plan
└─────────────┘                                │
  ┌ ─ ─ ↓↑ ─ ─ ─ ─ ─ ─ ─ ─ ─ ─ ─ ─ ─ ↓ ─ ┐
  │ ┌─────────────┐     ┌─────────────┐     │
  │ │ Objectives  │ ⇄  │ Initiatives │     │
  │ └─────────────┘     └─────────────┘     │
  │                           ↓             │
  │            ┌─────────────┐ ┌─────────────┐ │
  │            │    Tasks    │→│  Resources  │ │
  │            │             │ │  Required   │ │
  │            └─────────────┘ └─────────────┘ │
  └ ─ ─ ─ ─ ─ ─ ─ ─ ─ ─ ─ ─ ─ ─ ─ ─ ─ ─ ─ ┘
```

Monitoring and Measurement

Strategies and strategic plans are living documents and, as such, they must be monitored to gauge performance against the desired outcomes. If it is determined that environmental shifts, competitive pressures, political maneuvers, organizational changes, or other variables require that the strategy be adjusted to reflect new market realities and/or changing dynamics, the strategy should not be rigid, but instead, it should be adaptable.

To monitor the organization's performance and measure its plan execution, the organization must employ a performance monitoring & measurement system to help determine when adjustments to the plan are needed or when specific action plans have been successfully executed. The most common forms of monitoring & measurement tools are some form of a scorecard, tracking tool, project plan, or a simple spreadsheet.

THREE

THE CRITICAL NATURE OF BUSINESS INITIATIVES

• • •

NECESSARY CONDITIONS

W. Edwards Deming, a management consultant, Total Quality Management thought leader, and author of several seminal works on performance improvement, including the book *Quality, Productivity, and Competitive Position*, maintained that improvement is not possible without "profound knowledge," which comes from, among other things, an appreciation for "systems"—how they work, their deficiencies, their performance metrics, and what is required to improve them. Within this context, a system is defined as a collection of interrelated, interdependent components that act in concert to turn inputs into outputs in pursuit of a goal. Within this definition of a system is the idea that an organization—a business, an agency, a government, an institution—is just as much a system as mechanical devices or processes (which we commonly refer to as systems).

Systems exist to achieve some vision or accomplish a goal. In most cases, to accomplish a goal, the system (organization) must improve something related to the goal. For example, if an organization's goal is to become the #2 software provider in the Northeast Region of the United States, the organization must improve its sales performance, and software features, etc.; if an organization's goal is to become the industry leader in product quality, the organization must upgrade the performance of its product offerings toward its *desired outcome* of becoming the product-quality leader. In a complex system, such as an organization, it is not possible to simply jump from some current, undesired state to ... becoming the industry leader in product quality; a desired outcome.

Eliyahu M. Goldratt—a physicist and author of *The Goal: A Process of Ongoing Improvement*—argued that to move from some current non-optimized state to a future, desired outcome state, an organization must satisfy what he called "necessary conditions." According to Goldratt, a necessary condition is "a circumstance indispensable to some result, or that upon which everything is contingent." Within this definition is the inherent assumption of a prerequisite relationship between the goal one is attempting to achieve and the *necessary condition* to accomplish it. I interpret this to mean there must exist a cause-and-effect relationship between the goal and that which is necessary to accomplish the goal. In my experience, the necessary condition is the realization of initiatives related to business objectives. In other words, if an organization's managers cannot successfully execute an initiative that is necessary to achieve an associated business objective, then the organization will be unsuccessful in accomplishing the goal, which is determined by successful accomplishment of a related objective; no completed initiative means no achieved objective which means no accomplished goal.

CAUSALITY:
THE RELATIONSHIP BETWEEN GOALS, OBJECTIVES, AND INITIATIVES

Effective plans / strategies must contain relationships that follow cause-and-effect logic, eliminating coincidence as much as possible. Cause-and-effect supposes that if you do "A" then "B" will happen as a direct result of having done "A." If you do not do "A," however, then "B" will not happen.

Coincidence, on the other hand, supposes that if you do "C" then "D" happens. However, "D" could have happened even if you did not do "C." Therefore, the

"D" event would be considered a coincidence, because it randomly happened right after you did "C," and its occurrence was not related to or caused by "C."

An example of causation (cause-and-effect) is turning on a light switch: when you flip a light switch, the light comes on. If you flipped the switch 100 times, the light would come on 100 times. The light coming on (the effect) is a direct result of you having turned on the light switch—the *necessary condition* for the light coming on. And it is safe to assume that, if you did not turn on the light switch, then the light would not go on. Or it's like tipping dominoes: if you line up a row of ten dominoes with the *goal* of knocking down the tenth domino, and you tip the first domino into the second one, that initial tip (the cause) would ultimately result in the second, third, fourth, fifth ... and ultimately, the tenth domino falling down (the effect; the desired outcome).

Cause-and-effect considerations of strategy are concerned with performing actions to materialize theory. Strategy exists on two planes: *theory* and *activities*. When strategists plan, we attempt to understand theoretically the forces that bring about improvement and the nature of those forces. Simply put, we try to determine what causes what to happen, when it happens, and why it happens. From our understanding of the theoretical (cause-and-effect), we then attempt to determine the activities (necessary conditions) that will lead to the desired outcomes and determine what the organization actually *does*; theory precedes action.

The "if-then" nature of strategy holds that once we undertake an action, we expect that the outcome of the action (an outcome we predicted would occur before we took the action) actually occurs. In a well-developed plan, this cause-and-effect relationship will exist between goals and objectives; objectives and initiatives; and initiatives and tasks.

The Cause-and-Effect Relationships Between the Elements of a Strategy

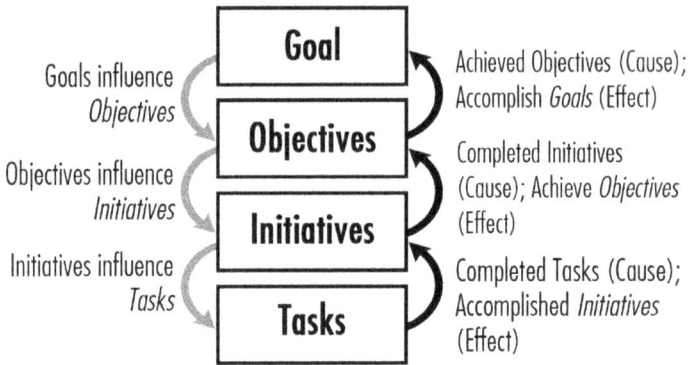

Goals influence *Objectives*	**Goal**	Achieved Objectives (Cause); Accomplish *Goals* (Effect)
Objectives influence *Initiatives*	**Objectives**	Completed Initiatives (Cause); Achieve *Objectives* (Effect)
Initiatives influence *Tasks*	**Initiatives**	Completed Tasks (Cause); Accomplished *Initiatives* (Effect)
	Tasks	

For example, if a goal is "To become the #2 software provider in the Northeast Region of the United States," and the objective that supports (determines the accomplishment of) the goal is to "Achieve $X + $1 in software sales by December 31st," then the *effect* of having achieved the objective will be goal accomplishment.

Plans that are developed without cause-and-effect relationships have been developed poorly, and their execution would not necessary equal progress toward achieving the plan's goals and objectives. It must be noted that, even if an organization gets the strategy "right" and even carries it out efficiently and effectively, all the organization can hope for is that the odds are in its favor that the strategy will be effectively executed, resulting in its desired outcomes.

Initiatives as Critical Success Factors (CSF)

Critical success factors (CSF) are the few key areas of activity in which successful completion are absolutely necessary for a manager to achieve her or his goals and objectives.

Necessary conditions not only have a supporting relationship with critical success factors, but they can also be considered critical success factors, because, as the name implies, such factors are *necessary* to achieve success; success being defined as the accomplishment of defined goals, objectives, and desired outcomes.

CSF represent the *factors* which are *critical* to the *success* of the manager charged with achieving certain objectives. Research shows that today's managers do an incredible number of different "things" in the course of a single day, things to which her attention can be diverted. The key to success for most managers is to focus their most limited resource (their time) on those things which make a difference between success and failure— success defined by the achievement of objectives and failure being the inability to achieve objectives. As I wrote previously: any activities in which a manager engages that do not directly support the organization's strategy are wasted efforts.

Question: Within the framework of a strategy, which elements are, in fact, the necessary conditions and/or critical success factors for an organization to accomplish its goals? The answer: **Initiatives**.

Initiatives are the things that must be completed or realized (the cause) for an objective to be achieved (the effect). As I wrote previously, a necessary condition is a circumstance indispensable to some result, or that upon which everything is contingent. Given this definition of a necessary condition as a *cause* for some result to occur, and the definition of a CSF as the factors necessary for success—with success being defined as objective accomplishment—then it stands to reason that strategy initiatives are, indeed, necessary and critical to successful objective achievement; they define the conditions that must occur and the factors that must be executed for objectives to be achieved, and ultimately goals, to be accomplished.

Referring back to my discussion of the cause-and-effect nature of the elements of a business-unit level strategy, the strategy's goals are the ultimate end: the desired outcome of executing the strategy. The way we know that a goal has been accomplished is by the successful achievement of the supporting objectives that collectively define goal-accomplishment; the satisfaction of the objectives lead to (cause) the fulfillment of the goal (effect).

Goal Accomplished	← Cause	Objectives Achieved

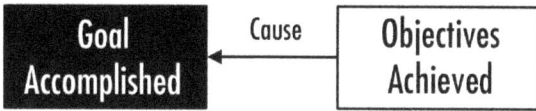

Goals cannot be accomplished without the successful achievement of their associated objectives, and objectives cannot be achieved without the successful realization of the initiatives whose completion is prerequisite to the achievement of their associated objectives. Continuing my previous example, if a goal is "To become the #2 software provider in the Northeast Region of the United States," and the objective that supports (determines the accomplishment of) the goal is to "Achieve $X + $1in software sales by December 31st," and, assume the ONLY way the company can achieve $X + $1 in software sales by December 31st is to win the competitive Acme Bank deal, then the initiative—the necessary condition to the software company achieving its $X + $1 sales objective—becomes "Win the Acme Bank deal"; it becomes the critical success factor.

Initiative as CSF

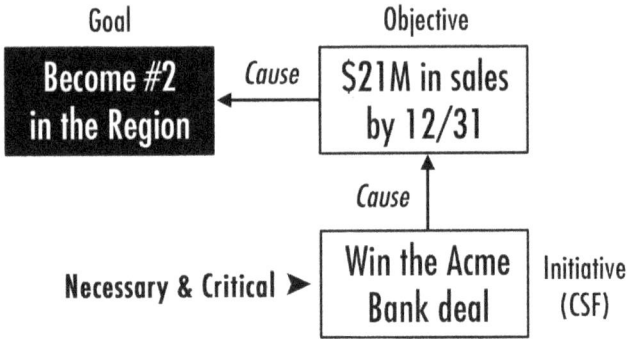

Goal		Objective
Become #2 in the Region	◄── *Cause*	**$21M in sales by 12/31**

Cause ▲

| **Necessary & Critical** ➤ | **Win the Acme Bank deal** | Initiative (CSF) |

To be sure, there is hardly ever only one way to achieve an objective; in the example above, there could potentially be several ways for the organization to achieve $X + $1 in software sales within the desired timeframe. In such cases, there would be multiple initiatives the organization could try to execute toward that end. Even in such instances, the organization would develop a set of initiatives applying cause-and-effect logic such that initiative realization is necessary—and critical to the successful outcome or achieving the $X + $1 sales objective and accomplishing the goal of becoming the #2 software provider in the region. Without initiatives, the objective would not be possible to achieve.

Initiative as CSF

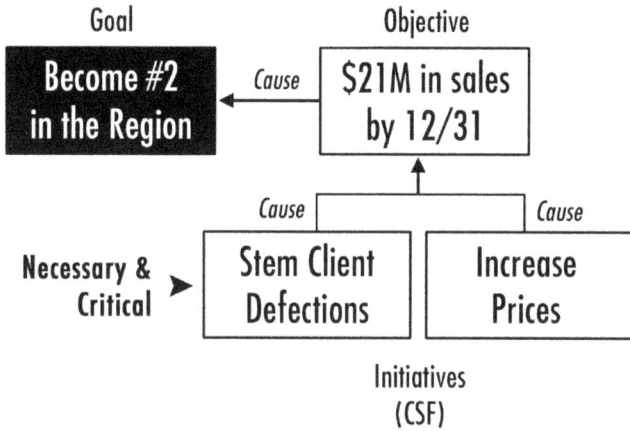

Goal		Objective

```
┌──────────────┐         ┌──────────────┐
│  Become #2   │  Cause  │ $21M in sales│
│ in the Region│ ◄────── │   by 12/31   │
└──────────────┘         └──────────────┘
                                 ▲
              Cause   ┌──────────┴──────────┐   Cause
  Necessary &    ┌─────────────┐     ┌─────────────┐
   Critical   ►  │ Stem Client │     │  Increase   │
                 │ Defections  │     │   Prices    │
                 └─────────────┘     └─────────────┘
                          Initiatives
                            (CSF)
```

A point about business objectives: In addition to being specific to the goal, clearly-defined, and measurable, objectives should be realistically achievable, otherwise, the pursuit of the objective could be a futile waste of time and destined for failure. Such a failure would negatively impact an organization's performance. For instance, one would not base an organization's survival on a plan with unrealistic odds of success; it would be like basing an organization's revenue objectives on winning the lottery: futile.

A lottery (often referred to as "LOTTO") is a game of chance where a player selects six (6) numbers from a field of 40 or more numbers. If these six numbers match the six drawn LOTTO draw numbers, the player wins a prize. In the United States, lotteries are subject to the laws of each jurisdiction, so there is no national lottery as there is in some countries, only state-wide lotteries. The biggest jackpot in U.S. lottery history was $636 million; it was won in 2012.

Such gargantuan prize winnings can be life-changing, and millions of people each year purchase tickets for a chance to partake in the bounty. There is only one way to win the jackpot, by picking 6 numbers correctly from a field of 40. The odds of correctly picking the six drawn numbers and winning the jackpot are one in 3.83 million. A person would have better odds of getting a royal flush in poker on the first five cards dealt (649,740 to 1), being killed by lightning (2.3 million to 1), dating a supermodel—men or women (88,000 to 1), or getting a hole in one (5,000 to 1).

If a person in 2012 established a goal to become "rich," and an associated objective to make $636 million by winning the LOTTO, such an objective would be unrealistic because (1) the six numbers chosen are out of the person's control—their direct efforts of choosing six random numbers would not result in these numbers becoming the six winning numbers—and (2) the 3.83 million to one odds of winning the lottery are too prohibitive for anyone to build a realistic plan around it; the person's odds of achieving the $636 million wealth objective and, therefore, his goal of becoming "rich" is virtually zero—or, more precisely, one in 3.83 million. This means that the person will have a better chance of gaining a (modest) financial windfall by robbing Bank of America; the odds of success are better at approximately 67%. In the end, the person using the lottery as his means of becoming rich is wasting his time and money.

The major challenge with establishing unattainable objectives like winning $636 million in the lottery is that there can be no cause-and-effect relationships (with at least 95% confidence that "if I do A, then B will result") between completing an initiative (e.g. randomly picking six numbers and playing the LOTTO) and achieving the associated objective (winning $636 million). My MBI proposition assumes such a relationship exists.

FOUR

MANAGEMENT BY INITIATIVES
(MBI)

• • •

An organization's leaders are measured on how "well" they run the organization; their performance. Exactly how a leader's performance is measured and the criteria on which the measurement is based can vary greatly from one organization to the next, depending on such factors as: the industry in which the organization operates; whether the organization is in the private or public sector; the condition of the organization when the leader joins; the environment in which the business operates; whether the organization is privately-held or publicly traded; and other factors. In most organizations—specifically in the private sector—the performance of an organization's leaders is measured against some established performance criteria. Whether it's quantitative metrics such as earnings growth, stock performance, earnings per share, sales targets, and market share growth, or qualitative metrics such as customer satisfaction, management "style," or some combination of all of the above, whatever the approach, the operative term used when gauging a leader's performance is performance *measurement.*

Measurement is a vehicle used to ascertain the degree to which one's performance meets some desired performance standard. What is implicit in this statement is that one's performance is based on metrics, which are parameters or measures of *quantitative* assessment used to track performance. Performance metrics are specific to an organization's purpose and directly related to its goals. But mostly, performance metrics are designed to measure success or failure.

When creating performance metrics, there are several factors to consider. In my experience, two of the most important questions to consider related to the development of useful performance metrics are:

- Can the performance metric be measured?

- Are there measurement milestone activities within each metric? Put differently, can the performance metric be made actionable?

Every organization wants to improve its performance. To upgrade performance, you must be able to measure the existing performance level. Measurement requires metrics and metrics should be made quantitative, otherwise there can be subjectivity as to whether or not a performance metric was satisfactorily achieved. For example, "customer satisfaction" as a metric is subjective and its provision open to debate. If, for instance, a manager was charged with "increasing customer satisfaction" and at performance-review time, the manager claimed that s/he improved customer satisfaction while the manager's boss believed otherwise, the review could quickly become unproductive. For reasons such as this, I always recommend to leaders of firms that have customer satisfaction as a performance metric or even a desired goal, that they convert customer satisfaction and other qualitative targets to a quantitative measure (where possible).

THE RELATIONSHIP BETWEEN PERFORMANCE AND EXECUTION

Performance is based on strategy execution

One of the major challenges facing organizations in their pursuit of improvement through strategy is translating strategy into actual performance. Performance improvement is based on plan execution, meaning, achieving some set of desired outcomes—goals and objectives. When organizations perform poorly for reasons other than executive inattention, their leaders often cannot determine whether the strategy was bad, whether the strategy was not executed effectively, neither of the above, or some combination thereof. When the strategy is not or cannot be effectively translated into specific action plans (initiatives and tasks—including accountability and the appropriate allocation of resources necessary to complete the tasks in the desired timeframes—designed to achieve measurable objectives), I have found that strategy execution is poor and, consequently, performance toward achieving the expected results is far below expectations.

EXECUTION IS THE ACHIEVEMENT of desired outcomes—usually goals and objectives—through specific, aligned activities. When it comes to extracting benefits from a strategy, execution is the key. The reason is execution is the "how" to the strategy's "what," and, in the case of strategy, the "what" is rendered useless if it is not realized through the "how."

In the culinary world, a recipe is a set of instructions used for preparing and producing a certain food, dish, or drink. The purpose of a recipe is to achieve a desired outcome, say, to produce a cake so delicious that it wins the Pillsbury Bake-Off Contest. The recipe lists all ingredients in the order they will be added, the amount of each ingredient to be used, and the preparation instructions.

When a chef creates a cake recipe and writes it down, if the recipe never gets made into an actual cake, then having the documented recipe will never enable the chef to win the Pillsbury Bake-Off Contest. In this case, as it relates to the chef accomplishing his goal of winning the contest, the recipe without execution is useless. In this example, the recipe is the strategy; it is the *what*, as in: here is *what* needs to be done to bake an award-winning cake. The actual act of baking the cake is the initiative; it is the *how*, as in: here is *how* we will produce an award-worthy cake and present it to the judges.

In the "what versus how" paradigm, *what* represents the requirements, or the goals the organization is to accomplish if it is to prosper, and *how* represents implementation (execution) of the strategy designed to achieve the goals and objectives.

Using the example of the Pillsbury Bake-Off Contest as a metaphor:

- The recipe is the strategy, and baking the cake is execution.
- Winning the Bake-Off Contest is the goal, and baking the cake is the initiative.

Strategies provide little value (but typically waste a lot of time and money) if they are developed and filed away in a desk drawer without ever being executed. If an organization has a genuine desire to deliver value, create a sustainable competitive advantage, or simply to accomplish a goal—and they develop a strategy toward those ends—then I contend that **executing the strategy initiatives** provides the most impact toward realizing one's goals and objectives. The reason is because *the initiatives, more than any other element of the strategy, define in actionable terms the things that must be done to achieve the objectives around which the initiatives are aligned.* Only by achieving the strategy's objectives can the strategy's goals be accomplished. For this reason, I refer to initiatives as a strategy's *Execution Point.*

INITIATIVES: THE EXECUTION POINT

The Execution Point of a strategy is the point that binds the theoretical (the *what*) elements of a strategy (its goals and objectives) to the actionable (the *how*) elements of the strategy (its initiatives and tasks). It is the point where theory becomes practical, where ideas become real, where the plan gets put into practice, where the recipe becomes a cake. Initiatives answer these questions:

- How will we achieve the objectives?
- What must we do to deliver the quantitative targets defined in the objectives within the defined timeframes?
- How will we know that the activities or projects in which we engage result in the achievement of quantifiable, measurable, time-specific objective criteria?

A strategy cannot be effectively executed without answers to these questions; these questions define initiatives. Therefore, a strategy cannot succeed without well-articulated initiatives.

The cause-and-effect nature of strategy demands that the initiatives that are defined in response to these questions will, if realized completely, satisfy the requirements of the objective to which the initiatives are linked: If we successfully "do" the initiatives, then we will have achieved the objective.

Some may argue that since the strategy's tasks define the specific action items (the work) needed to complete an initiative, the tasks should be considered the Execution Point. Others may argue that, since the objectives are the measurable manifestation of goals, the objectives are the most important strategy element. To be certain, tasks and objectives are critical elements of any strategy; nothing gets accomplished without the work (tasks) being performed, and, in most cases, goals have no practical meaning if not made practical by their supporting objectives. Yet, the objectives are mostly useless unless made actionable by the initiatives, and the tasks would have no guidance (the task owners would not know what to do) and cannot begin until the initiative which defines their actions is first developed. Without initiatives, the strategy cannot be executed.

When you consider the strategy as a whole and the amount of resources and effort that goes into the strategy process, a small amount (approximately 10%) of the effort and resources are invested in strategy development. The majority of the strategy effort and resources (the other 90%) are required to execute the strategy. Execution is critical to performance, it is where competitive advantages are either gained or lost. And the linchpin of both the strategy and the execution effort is the initiatives.

Initiatives are where the strategic meets the tactical action plane. Goals are manifest as measurable objectives; objectives dictate initiatives and cannot be achieved without successful completion of the associated initiatives; initiatives dictate the tasks and action that define the specific steps that must be taken to complete an initiative; and resource requirements (including human resources) are determined by the tasks that are to be completed as part of the action plan which is influenced by the strategy initiatives. If you remove the initiatives from a strategic plan, the plan will not be successful. Therefore, **initiatives are *critical success factors*.**

The Execution Point

Performance is where execution leads to desired outcomes;
where realized initiatives result in the achievement of objectives

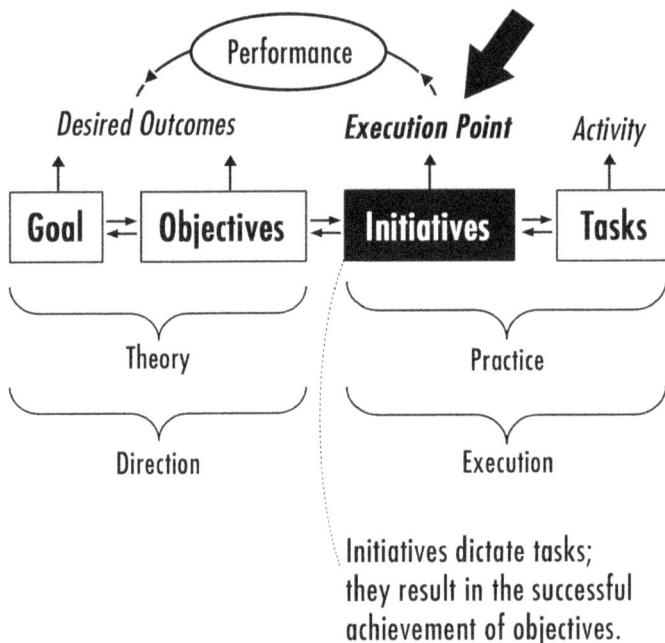

Performance

Desired Outcomes   *Execution Point*   *Activity*

| Goal | ⇄ | Objectives | ⇄ | Initiatives | ⇄ | Tasks |

Theory   Practice

Direction   Execution

Initiatives dictate tasks;
they result in the successful
achievement of objectives.

A HISTORICAL PERSPECTIVE ON MANAGING BY INITIATIVES

An early indication of the need for business-unit leaders to focus their efforts on strategic initiatives toward strategy execution and better organizational performance can be gleaned from a historical investigation of the formative days of American enterprise.

Before 1850, very few American businesses required any type of formal organizational structure. In those days, companies were very small, usually family-run operations compared with today's industrial organizations. The businesses were very flat, with no vertical reporting structures or different departments to speak of. The few business owners or business executives who were responsible for corporate prosperity handled all of the business functions, including: financial, administrative, and operational duties.

Over time, factors such as population growth, new wealth and prosperity, population shifts from the country to cities, and technology advancements created new and changing demands for a company's goods and services. The prospect of capturing revenue from a new market of users or to mitigate the threat of losing current market share to new competitors stimulated expansion, vertical integration, and product diversification. In response to the growing opportunities and increasing demands placed on companies due to population growth and increased household incomes, companies were forced to change their strategies, no matter how informal strategies were at the time. In many cases, planning for and capturing new growth were considered a strategy itself, which called for changes in business structure; growth without structural changes can lead to inefficiency.

In the early 1850s, the expansion and length of railroad lines facilitated population shifts and commerce, and increased the patronage of railroads (business growth requiring a new strategy) making the railroads the largest business enterprise in the United States, and their operation demanded new management approaches.

In 1855, Daniel McCallum, the General Superintendent of the Erie Rail Line, noted that:

> "Any system that might be applicable to the business and extent of a short road would be found entirely inadequate to the want of a long one; and I am fully convinced that in the want of a system perfect in its details, properly adapted and vigilantly enforced, lies the true secret of their failure; and that this disparity of cost per mile in operating long and short roads is not produced by a difference in length, but is in proportion to the perfection of the system adopted."

To McCallum, the "system adopted" meant a formal definition of the lines of authority and communication between the headquarters and field locations, which he illustrated. This illustration is credited as being the first formal organization chart by an American company. McCallum's organization chart idea was soon adopted by the other major U.S. railroad companies.

The significance of this development for the need for business-unit leaders to manage by initiatives is in the challenges brought on by formal organization structures with various roles and responsibilities in larger organizations. As organizations grew and began to diversify into decentralized organizations (what we know as multi-divisional organization types) where the central office plans, coordinates, and allocates resources (develops strategy) for the operating divisions, the need for business-unit leaders grew.

Executives who planned and allocated resources became key organizational figures and their decisions and actions were considered entrepreneurial. Managers, on the other hand, were responsible for *operating* decisions and actions, meaning carrying out (executing) the plans using the resources allocated to them by the organization's executives. Strategy is about deciding on which things the organization should do and operations is about doing them; operating decisions relate to execution.

In those earlier times, although executives made some of the most important decisions in history, they were not universally interested in long-term strategic planning. In many organizations, executives responsible for planning and resource allocation concentrated on day-to-day operational activities while ignoring such things as changing market forces and other more strategic, forward-thinking issues. In other words, they acted like managers. Executives who actually guided organizational activities and cared about future growth and other long-range issues presided over enterprises that performed better than those who did not.

As Alfred D. Chandler wrote in his classic book *Chapters in the History of the American Industrial Enterprise* when reflecting on his research findings:

> "In planning and coordinating the work of subordinate managers or supervisors, [the executive] allocates tasks and makes available the necessary equipment, materials, and other physical resources necessary to carry out the various jobs. In appraising their activities, he must decide whether the employees or subordinate managers are handling their tasks satisfactorily. If not, he can take action …"

In this context, "satisfactorily" handling the *tasks* meant effectively completing the tasks which the manager had been assigned. Within a strategy, every task is related to and completed toward the realization of the initiative which dictates the need for the tasks to be completed. This is logical when you consider that, in order for an executive to validate "satisfactory" task completion, the tasks must be specified, and for a task to be specific, it must be specific to the achievement of some desired outcome. Tasks are dictated by and performed in support of initiatives; no manager should simply perform random tasks with no relation to the organization's strategy, or it is wasted effort. Within a strategy, the way that tasks relate to and support the strategy is through the initiatives which the tasks are defined to realize; the initiative is the lifeblood of tasks. So, if the manager's performance will be judged based on his or her successful completion of tasks, and—as I have made clear within this text—tasks are fundamentally collective activities performed to realize an initiative, then, consequently, the manger's performance will be judged based on the *collective* of his or her tasks: the strategic initiatives; the *Execution Point*.

Initiatives
The Lifeblood of Tasks

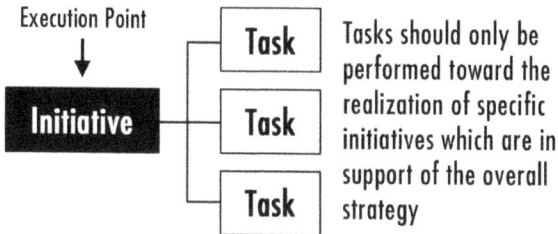

Tasks should only be performed toward the realization of specific initiatives which are in support of the overall strategy

THE IMPORTANCE OF
REALIZING INITIATIVES

Within a strategy, the goals define the way forward, the objectives define the metrics that indicate successful goal accomplishment, and the initiatives answer the most significant questions related to strategy execution: *how will the objectives be achieved* or *what must we do to successfully meet or exceed the metrics defined by the objec-*

tives? Without answers to these fundamental questions, an organization will waste time, money, and other resources doing "things" that may have no bearing on the success of their strategy, thereby decreasing the chances of receiving the benefits the strategy was designed to produce; strategy initiatives provide the answers, and the business-unit leaders are responsible for executing initiatives.

It's one thing to say or propose that business-unit leaders must focus their efforts on realizing initiatives if strategies are to have the greatest chance of success, but it's wholly another to demonstrate it by asking three worker-related MBI planning questions:

1. What should workers in an organization *do?*

2. Why should the workers do what you suggest in your answer to question #1?

3. How will the workers know *what* to do to satisfy your answer to question #1?

Any business-unit leader who cannot answer these three basic planning questions is likely managing by the seat of his or her pants. And any business-unit leader who *can* answer these questions will most certainly answer question #3 with "the workers' activities will be directed at realizing initiatives toward accomplishing strategy goals." I will examine these questions in greater detail to shed light on the importance of workers' efforts being focused on initiatives.

QUESTION #1:
What should workers in an organization do?

In short, workers should perform *productive activities.* Productive activities are those which make things, bring something into existence, accomplish something particular, or *cause something to happen.*

In a capitalistic economic system, the basic labor-to-wealth model (discussed below) is common within a capitalistic enterprise:

1. The enterprise owner seeks capital wealth;

2. The owner identifies goods with "use-value" and "exchange-value";

3. The owner defines the processes to create and sell goods;

4. The owner hires workers to perform a task (labor) necessary to create and sell the goods, ultimately delivering wealth;

5. The labor is divided by skill, and workers follow the defined processes to produce and sell the goods. The *division of labor* is a specific mode of cooperation wherein different tasks are assigned to different people based on the tasks needed to produce a specific good;

6. The goods, which have "use-value," are sold to buyers. A "use-value" means that a good must have properties that allow it to satisfy some human need or want;

7. Buyers pay the owners for the goods which have an "exchange-value" (worth exchange for something of equal value, e.g. money); and

8. The owner of the goods acquires capital wealth.

Labor in this model is hired to perform *productive work*: work that produces goods with *use-value* and *exchange-value*. In *Capital: A Critique of Political Economy*, German philosopher Karl Marx wrote that productive activity (which he called "the useful character of the labor"), is simply the expenditure of human labor power performing qualitatively different productive activities.

"Productive activity" begets productivity, the application of labor to bring about some desired outcome (goals). Productive activity is activity (a worker's labor) contributing to the achievement of business objectives and the accomplishment of business goals. In a capitalistic system, that goal is most often what Marx calls "capitalist wealth." He wrote:

> The utility of a thing makes it a use-value. The use values, coat, linen, etc., *i.e.*, the bodies of commodities, are combinations of two elements – matter and labor. In the use value of each commodity there is contained useful labor, *i.e.*, productive activity of a definite kind and <u>exercised with a definite aim</u>.

The coat, in this example, is a use-value item that satisfies a particular want. Its existence is the result of a worker's productive activity, the nature of which is determined by its aim. Put differently, workers' activities are determined by definite goals.

Because workers' activities are determined by goals, worker goal setting becomes critical in ensuring that workers' activities are not wasted efforts, but are, instead, laser-focused on producing desired results. Goal setting means:

- Clarifying what workers must do to help the organization "succeed" (defined by the organization's goals);
- Reducing ambiguity in a person's work;
- Reducing effort duplication;
- Establishing a relationship between a worker's work and organizational achievements;
- Providing a sense of accomplishment and personal fulfillment;
- Measuring performance; and
- Ensuring activities are directed toward accomplishing the organization's goals.

The Worker as a Business-Unit Leader:
"One Head, One Plan"

French industrialist Henry Fayol developed management theories and principles, which are universally accepted by management educators and practitioners of all stripes. He believed that organizational performance is facilitated when—among his other management principles—there is "unity of direction" within the organization and a "spirit of cooperation."

Under his *unity of direction* and *spirit of cooperation* principles, Fayol advocated that, within an organization, there should be "one head and one plan," meaning that group efforts toward strategic plan satisfaction should be led and directed by a single person—the manager or unit leader. He also advocated that the best results would be achieved when individual and group efforts are integrated and coordinated. He reasoned that unity of direction and cooperation would enable the effective coordination of individual efforts throughout an organization, leading to the *attainment of a common goal.*

An effective strategy is the vehicle that drives the alignment of work-related thought and effort among all organization members—assuming that all members are charged with work activities and responsibilities directed toward the satisfaction of the organization's goals and objectives. At the organization's business-unit level, the "one head" described in Fayol's Principles of Management is the business-unit leader, whose primary responsibilities are defined in the objectives and initiatives of the organization's strategic plan. The only way the business-unit leader can positively impact the business objectives that s/he is charged with achieving—or, at least, contributing to their achievement—is by realizing the initiatives for which s/he has been assigned responsibility to deliver.

The business-unit leader (the "one head") can only contribute to achieving business objectives by realizing business initiatives. **Objective-achievement is a natural offshoot of having realized the initiatives**; it will happen if the initiatives are successfully fulfilled. Therefore, the only effort the business-unit leader can expend toward objective achievement is toward the realization of *actionable* initiatives. I emphasize that the *initiatives* are actionable because objectives are *not*; they are the result of successfully-realized initiatives. This is illustrated in the diagram below.

Strategy Relationships

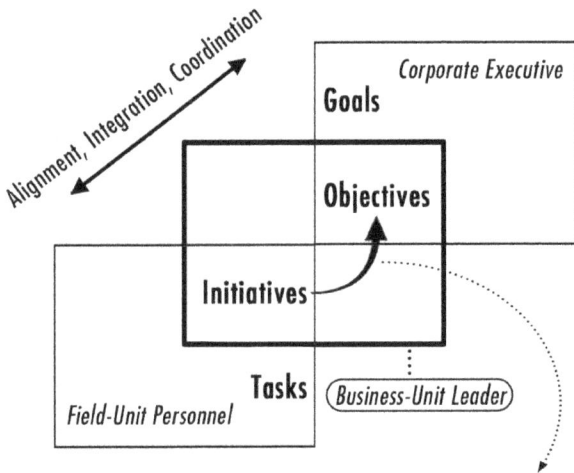

Goals — Corporate Executive

Objectives

Initiatives

Tasks — (Business-Unit Leader)

Field-Unit Personnel

Alignment, Integration, Coordination

The business-unit leader can only fulfill the objectives by realizing the initiatives. Achievement of the objectives is a natural result of realizing the initiatives.

QUESTION #2:

Why should the workers do what you suggest in your answer to question #1?

The simple answer is because they are *paid* for their labor. Payment—if the wage is fair—is an equitable exchange for their labor. Another reason, to a slightly lesser degree, is because work provides them with a sense of accomplishment, something that is important to the human psyche.

Americans who are not in the workforce are the most likely to be depressed. That's the conclusion of a 2013 survey conducted by the *Gallup-Healthways Well-Being Index*. It found that 16.6% of unemployed Americans are depressed compared with 5.6% of those who work full time. Gallup controlled for 12 variables: age, gender, income, education, race and ethnicity, marital status, having children, region, employment status, obesity, having health insurance, and being a caregiver, so that they could examine each factor independently to find out which is most strongly linked to depression.

"Self-esteem and self-worth are closely aligned with working," says psychotherapist Charles Allen, author of *Why Good People Make Bad Choices*. When you have a job, you are a contributing member of society, which gives you a sense of value and self-worth. This is consistent with psychologist Abraham Maslow's hierarchy of needs, which argues that people will be unfulfilled until they have satisfied basic physiological needs such as hunger, important needs such as safety & security (including work), and "esteem needs" which can come from achievement and the respect of others.

So, to remain gainfully-employed and to continue receiving the fulfilling benefits that employment can help bring, it is requisite that the worker performs the tasks that s/he has been hired to perform, and to perform them outstandingly.

QUESTION #3:
How will the workers know what to do to satisfy your answer to question #1?

Workers are hired to perform specific tasks related to that which the employer is trying to accomplish. In this case, if the employer is ultimately trying to increase her wealth and the means of wealth creation for this employer is the production and sale of goods, then the worker will be hired to perform a specific task related to the production or sale of goods.

What the worker must *specifically* do is determined by the processes that were defined to produce and sell the goods which are necessary for the capitalist to accomplish her goal of accumulating wealth. In the simplistic labor-to-wealth model previously introduced and restated below, the stage of the process where workers learn exactly what they must do in the performance of their job is at stage #5 where *workers follow the defined processes to produce and sell the goods.*

1. The enterprise owner seeks capital wealth;

2. The owner identifies goods with "use-value" and "exchange-value";

3. The owner defines the processes to create and sell goods;

4. The owner hires workers to perform a task (labor) necessary to create and sell goods, ultimately delivering wealth;

5. **Labor is divided by skill, and workers follow the defined processes to produce and sell the goods.** The *division of labor* is a specific mode of cooperation wherein different tasks are assigned to different people based on the tasks needed to produce a specific good;

6. The goods, which have "use-value," are sold to buyers. A "use-value" means that a good must have properties that allow it to satisfy some human need or want;

7. Buyers pay the owners for the goods which have an "exchange-value" (worth the exchange for something of equal value, e.g. money); and

8. The owner of the goods acquires capital wealth.

Ultimately, and in the strictest sense, the workers' activities have been specifically determined for the purpose of contributing to the owner's ultimate aim or goal, and nothing else.

The Relationship Between Workers' Activities and the Accomplishment of the Firm's Goals

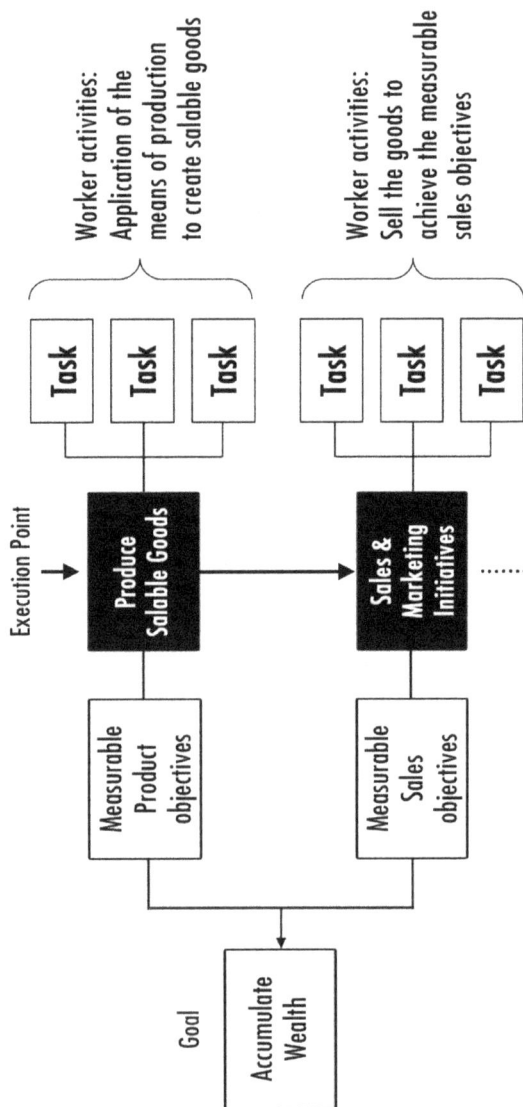

Worker activities: Application of the means of production to create salable goods

Worker activities: Sell the goods to achieve the measurable sales objectives

Execution Point

Task
Task
Task

Task
Task
Task

Produce Salable Goods

Sales & Marketing Initiatives

Measurable Product objectives

Measurable Sales objectives

Goal

Accumulate Wealth

In an organization, the executive (the strategist) would answer the three worker-related Management by Initiatives planning questions as follows:

Question #1: What should workers in an organization do?

If the worker is hired by an organization and paid an honest wage to perform the specific activities defined by the organization's leaders to support organizational goals, the worker should engage in activities *productively*. Productive activity denotes contributing to the achievement of objectives and goal accomplishment.

Question #2: Why should the workers do what you suggest in your answer to question #1?

Workers should perform the specific activities defined by the organization because they are paid (an assumptive honest wage) for their labor, for engaging in productive activity on behalf of the organization. To a lesser degree, workers should engage in productive work for a sense of accomplishment and the sense of fulfillment that work can provide.

Question #3: How will the workers know what to do to satisfy your answer to question #1?

The organization's strategy—and, as it directly relates to workers, the strategic initiatives—define the specific activities to be performed by the worker toward the satisfaction of organizational goals.

For the betterment of the organization, business-unit leaders / managers should be measured based on their performance, and performance is a function of execution. Therefore, a manager's performance should be based on their ability to execute elements of the strategy that result in *objective-achievement*, namely, its *initiatives*. Initiatives are realized when the tasks necessary to fulfill them are successfully accomplished by the organization's workers. For this reason, managers should spend time coaching, developing, and motivating workers toward the successful realization of initiatives.

EMPOWERING ASSOCIATES TO EXECUTE INITIATIVES

When organization leaders develop strategic plans and smartly foster plan alignment by driving the strategy through all organization levels and incorporating each person's strategy-related performance metrics into their performance plans, they create an environment of accountability at all levels of the organization for plan execution. As business-unit leaders and managers focus their efforts on realizing strategic initiatives and supporting objective achievement—their metrics in the performance plan—the business-unit leaders can ensure ongoing executive support and follow-through on commitments because the unit leaders will have an added incentive to do so since their job performance (via the performance plan review process) will be based on it. This intense focus on initiatives/objectives by unit leaders will, out of necessity, ensure focus and attention on the strategy by the organization's leaders. This is positive, because executive inattention to strategy is one of the primary reasons many strategies fail to deliver on expected outcomes.

When business-unit leaders, functional leaders, managers, and even their subordinates are held responsible for achieving performance measures that, in most cases, require the ability to make autonomous decisions to meet expectations, these personnel must be empowered to do so by the organization's leaders. One of the most significant factors in strategy success or failure is the power of the organization's people to act independently, and how well that power is focused toward meeting organizational objectives.

In the 1980s, Human Resource Management as a discipline began to flourish and management thinkers, including Rosabeth Moss Kanter and others, began to demonstrate that an organization's human resources— its people—were the most valuable organizational resource, and that involving them in the strategic planning process could enhance employee motivation, and thus, performance.

Deming claimed that the involvement and participation of employees at all levels is critical and that organizations should utilize all employees' skills and abilities to upgrade business performance. He referred to this participation as *Employee Involvement* (EI), a process of empowering employees to participate in managerial decision-making, including strategic planning.

In many instances, organizations treat EI as a strategic initiative to be realized in support of achieving business objectives. In the early 1980s, the Harley-Davidson Motor Company was facing bankruptcy. The economic recession, strong competition from Japanese manufacturers, and a prolonged history of declining quality were bringing the company to its proverbial knees.

By 1981, Harley-Davidson's quality problems began to override image-based sales and sales slid as Japanese competitors began to focus their efforts on the heavyweight motorcycle market. During that year, Harley's sales fell 18 percent and its U.S. market share in the once-dominant heavyweight bike class fell 5 percent, dipping below Honda's.

In this period, more than half of Harley's bikes failed inspection off the assembly line whereas only 5 percent of Japanese bikes failed. In an effort to improve quality, increase sales, and regain market share, Harley-Davidson decided to mimic the Japanese manufacturing processes which, incidentally, the Japanese had learned from American Edward Deming in the 1940s. Deming's strategy was based on three productivity improvement *initiatives*; one being Employee Involvement, through which Harley's leaders empowered its employees.

Harley-Davidson sought to dissolve the distinction between blue-collar and white-collar workers, facilitating joint working relationships. All workers with responsibility for achieving specific performance metrics were given decision-making authority, and managers were charged with having laser-like focus on achieving quantitative objective measures; in other words, managers were charged with realizing the EI initiative by achieving various business objectives identified by the company, including cost reduction.

By the end of 1982, costs had dropped significantly as a result of the focus on Harley's new initiatives, so much so, that the company needed to sell only 35,000 bikes to break even, as compared with the 53,000 bike breakeven point in 1980.

FIVE

CASE STUDY:
A BOTCHED 'PREMIER'

• • •

"Dear Fellow Employees and Retirees:

It is with great pride that I present to you Premier— the incredible new R.J. Reynolds Tobacco Co. cigarette that heats but does not burn tobacco.

Premier provides a cleaner smoke for smokers and those around them. … And through a remarkable technological breakthrough that made Premier possible, many of the controversial compounds found in the smoke of tobacco-burning cigarettes have been substantially reduced."

These were the words of R.J. Reynolds Tobacco Company Chairman and Chief Executive Officer Edward A. Horrigan, Jr. in a 1987 note to the company's employees that was included with a sample of its new cigarette brand, 'Premier,' the company's proposed solution for sagging cigarette sales.

The Premier brand cigarette was an early "smokeless" cigarette manufactured and marketed by R.J. Reynolds (RJR) in 1988. The development of the cigarette was known inside RJR as super-secret "Project SPA"; it was RJR's attempt to create a non-combustible cigarette to address health issues surrounding traditional cigarettes and secondhand smoke.

World tobacco sales for 1988 were $7.1 billion, up 11% from 1987. However, this increase was due to higher selling prices and strong international unit volume growth. RJR's domestic sales in 1988 showed a 9% increase from 1987. However, the increase resulted from higher selling prices which offset a 4% decline in domestic unit volume growth and a decrease in inventory turnover from 10.0 to 3.9. So, while the company's global tobacco sales rose between 1987 and 1988, the numbers masked a major challenge facing R.J. Reynolds: how to grow domestic volume.

At the time, Philip Morris' (a major competitor) market share was increasing a percentage point each year, whereas RJR's share had stagnated. According to Reynolds spokeswoman Betsy Annese, "We are predicting about a 1 to 1.5 percent volume decline for the industry per year," she said. The impact of the tobacco sales volume decline on RJR was manifest in the company's 1987 decision to reduce its domestic work force by 2,800 employees; the domestic market was, in fact, the market in which RJR's tobacco volume had been declining over the years. This was supported by statements from corporate executives who cited a decreased demand for cigarettes and a tougher tobacco marketplace for its decision to cut work force.

Responding to increased competitive pressures and shrinking domestic volume growth, RJR responded with a four-pronged strategy:

- Differentiate its products;
- Diversify into non-cigarette products;
- Focus on overseas markets (where cigarette growth was increasing at double-digit rates); and
- Address increasing health concerns in the U.S. This was, as it is today, a major threat to the tobacco industry.

An important accomplishment in the second half of the 20th century has been the reduction in smoking rates among people aged 18 and older from 42.4% in 1965 to approximately 33.7% in 1988. In addition, the percentage of adults who have never smoked cigarettes increased steadily from the mid-1960s.

The smoking reduction can be attributed to many factors, including: scientific evidence of the relationship among disease, tobacco use, and environmental exposure to tobacco; dissemination of this information to the public; an increase in prevention and cessation programs; campaigns by advocates for nonsmokers' rights; restrictions on cigarette advertising; counter-advertising; policy changes (i.e., enforcement of laws restricting minors' access, legislation restricting smoking in public places, and increased taxation); improvements in treatment and prevention programs; and an increased understanding of the economic costs of tobacco.

As anti-smoking measures increased and competitors' market share climbed, R.J. Reynolds—always an industry pioneer—sought to gain a competitive advantage and drive tobacco volume growth by investing $325 million in a cigarette product that addressed some of the major public concerns about cigarette smoke, including the carcinogenic nature of cigarette smoke and the dangers of second-hand smoke to non-smokers. The answer, they believed, was the Premier cigarette.

Billed as "the cleaner smoke," Premier was a mechanical cigarette not significantly unlike the Electronic Cigarettes (e-Cigarettes) of today. Reynolds touted Premier as a "cleaner" cigarette—which was supposed to give consumers the impression that the cigarette was safer than typical cigarettes—because it produced no smoke from the tip and no ashes.

For many reasons, including the cigarette's smell and taste (it had been reported that R.J. Reynolds' CEO Edward Horrigan had smoked a Premier cigarette and complained that it "tasted like shit"); the cigarette's difficult usability; the device's public image as being useful as a potential crack cocaine pipe; and the need to cut costs because of the leveraged buyout of Reynolds' parent, RJR Nabisco Inc., the company eventually abandoned the Premier cigarette project. A closer inspection of the Premier cigarette initiative provides insight into the negative impact that RJR's lack of effective focus on this strategic initiative had on the cigarette's go-to-market aspirations.

AN EXAMINATION OF THE R.J. REYNOLDS' PREMIER STRATEGY

While we understand the reasons why Premier failed to meet the company's expectations from a causality standpoint, one question remains: Where—if anywhere—in Premier's strategy did evidence exist that the brand would be a failure?

The company had clearly defined a major goal of *improving tobacco volume growth*. Improvement is about making changes that will lead the company in a new direction, and the improvement process begins by answering five fundamental improvement-related questions. The questions are listed below, in addition to answers that have been informed by my research into the case.

1. *What are you trying to accomplish*? Prior to the 1988 $26 billion leveraged buyout of RJR Nabisco by

Kohlberg, Kravis and Roberts (KKR), R.J. Reynolds wanted, most importantly among other things, to grow its tobacco share and sales volume (not simply dollar sales growth). The domestic sales volume had been steadily declining and the company wanted to reverse that course and improve its competitive positioning.

2. *What's broken and how do we know it's broken?* For RJR, domestic tobacco sales volume was down approximately 4% from 1987. The company was losing market share to its key competitor Philip Morris, and the number of existing and "new" smokers—RJR's growth targets—had been steadily declining since 1965.

3. *What do we want to change (do differently)?* RJR wanted to create a product (Premier) that would address the cigarette-related health concerns of both smokers and non-smokers alike; a product that would steal concerned existing smokers away from its competitors and attract new, younger people to become RJR cigarette brand smokers.

4. *How will you know that a change is an improvement?* My analysis revealed that, unfortunately for RJR, the company did not have an effective causality-based strategy to ensure that its actions (Premier development and marketing) resulted in the company's desired outcomes (tobacco sales volume growth and market share increase). In other words, RJR had very

little confidence, assurance, or proof that the activities in which they engaged when they went to market with Premier would directly result in the company's desired outcomes.

5. *What changes can you make that will result in an improvement?* Effective strategies must contain relationships that follow cause-and-effect logic. Cause-and-effect supposes that if you do "A" then "B" will happen as a direct result of having done "A." One RJR goal was *to grow tobacco sales volume*; one of the objectives that supported (ensured the achievement of) the goal was *to increase U.S. market share*; one of the initiatives supporting the objective was *to develop and market Premier*; and the specific tasks supporting initiative-completion should have been defined in such a way that ensured (or at least provided a high probability of success of) initiative-completion, which would have ensured the achievement of the related objective, which would have contributed to successful accomplishment of the goal to grow tobacco sales volume.

Following this logic, if RJR was successful at developing and marketing Premier, the company would have been successful at achieving its related objective—then the *effect* of having successfully completed the development and marketing of Premier.

The failure of Premier begs the question: What could R.J. Reynolds have done within the context of its volume growth strategy to increase the likelihood of a successful Premier cigarette launch? To address this issue, it is necessary to examine RJR's strategy for Premier.

The Premier Strategy

An examination of the market conditions and competitive forces surrounding RJR and the market for tobacco, its tobacco sales volume goals for the period in question, and the wealth of information related to the planning, launch, and dramatic failure of the Premier cigarette brand has allowed me to interpret and recreate the basic RJR strategic plan framework for Premier.

RJR Strategic Plan Framework: Premier

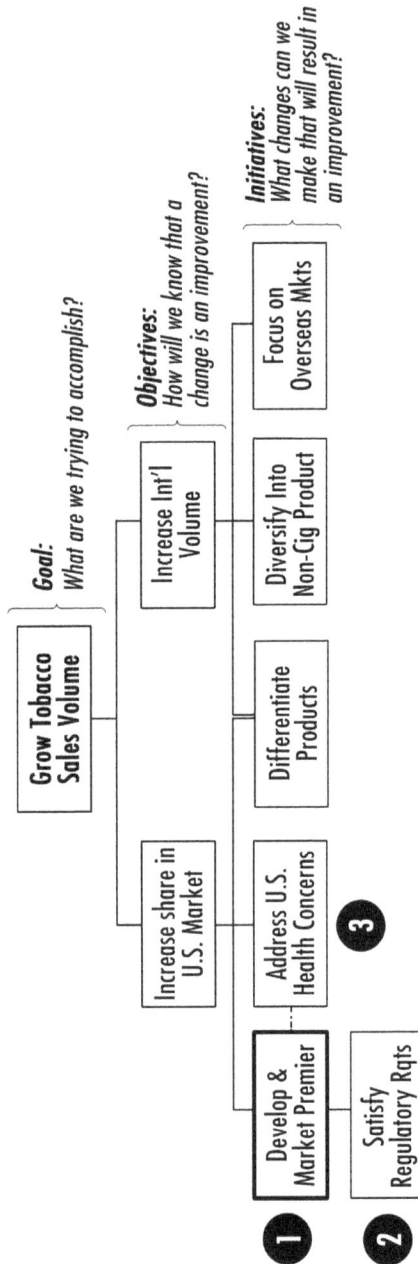

Goal:
What are we trying to accomplish?

Objectives:
How will we know that a change is an improvement?

Initiatives:
What changes can we make that will result in an improvement?

Grow Tobacco Sales Volume

Increase share in U.S. Market

Increase Int'l Volume

Differentiate Products

Diversify Into Non-Cig Product

Focus on Overseas Mkts

Address U.S. Health Concerns

Develop & Market Premier

Satisfy Regulatory Rqts

1

2

3

An examination of the Premier case reveals that the cigarette's failure was primarily driven by a failure to define and execute two key initiatives and the supporting tasks for one: (1) the development and go-to-market for the Premier brand; (2) the associated tasks for satisfying U.S. regulatory requirements for the non-traditional cigarette; and (3) address health concerns in the U.S. related to smoking and second-hand cigarette smoke.

[1] Initiative: Develop & Market Premier

The evidence suggests that RJR did a poor job of defining and executing the tasks that, if executed properly, would have resulted in the successful development and test market launch of Premier (the initiative).

My work with organizations globally on business-unit-level strategy development and consulting on existing strategies illustrates that the one area where organizations consistently fall short is at the initiative and task definition stages of the planning process. When defining initiatives to achieve their associated objective, and tasks to realize their associated initiatives, there are three fundamental questions that business-unit leaders must answer assuredly and honestly.

Questions for defining initiatives to support an objective:

1. What are all of the "things" that must be done to deliver the quantifiable metrics defined in the objective? [Develop a complete list of the potential proj-

ects or initiatives (not specific action items or *tasks*) that would lead to objective satisfaction].

2. If we successfully accomplish each of these "things" (initiatives, projects), are we at least 95% confident that we will, as a result, achieve the quantifiable metrics defined in the objective? [Before proceeding, the answer must be "Yes"].

3. How do we *know* that the successful accomplishment of each of the initiatives/projects will result in the successful achievement of the objective? [This question relates to the cause-and-effect nature of the objective-initiative relationship of the strategy].

When applying this model to the Premier launch and go-to-market, I found that it is highly unlikely that the Premier product development and marketing teams answered these question assuredly or thoroughly. The evidence for this can be found in the features & functions of the product itself, the target market demographic they pursued, and the blasé attitude they exhibited toward the U.S. Food and Drug Administration (FDA) related to Premier.

Premier's Features and Functions: The first clue that Premier could run into trouble occurred during product development, where the product's requirements determine what the developers build into the product. Premier's product management was responsible for, among other things, developing the product strategy and aligning it with Premier's defined sales objectives. This process involves—among the voluminous documentation required for a product development plan—the development of a business requirements document that defines solutions to the known cigarette-related problem facing RJR, and a product requirements document that incorporates the required features into the product. If these documents had been thoroughly developed, the product development team would have identified three critical characteristics of the Premier cigarette that must have been incorporated into the product's features & functions specs for the product to have had the best chance at being adopted: nicotine content, taste, and the cigarette "experience."

Nicotine Content: Nicotine is a powerfully addictive drug, and, like other addictive drugs, is the primary reason why cigarette smokers *must* have their cigarettes. The addiction requires that smokers maintain a serum nicotine level (the amount of nicotine in their blood stream) to avoid withdrawal symptoms and help the smoker relax. Smoking a cigarette with adequate nicotine content eases the discomfort of nicotine withdrawal. With Premier, even when properly lit, it was extremely difficult to draw nicotine or anything else out of the cigarette, which required, as one writer put it, "Herculean sucking capabilities."

Taste: RJR executives acknowledged that the Premier cigarette taste was an "acquired" taste. According to a 1947 study on the smoking habits of cigarette smokers, a person usually dislikes the taste of his first cigarette; the taste for cigarettes must be gradually acquired. Whenever a smoker tries a new brand with a different taste than their usual brand, the smoker finds that he must become accustomed to the taste. The study also found that smokers who say they do not like the taste of certain cigarette brands really mean that they are not accustomed to it. This is a finding that RJR discovered far too late in the product launch process.

The Premier cigarette was a "stationary furnace" device that operated by separating the combustion material (carbon) from the aerosol-generating material (mostly glycerol) so that the inhaled by-products yielded when smoked were the distillation products (glycerol and water), rather than the combustion products (nicotine and smoke constituents) as in traditional cigarettes. The flavoring was derived from tobacco, nicotine, the paper roll, and a sprayed dried extract. Additional flavors (raspberry and chocolate) were also added to enhance the tobacco taste and give Premier a "pleasing aroma" in the smoke. This added flavor was a major reason that Premier failed in the test market as the taste was radically different from conventional cigarettes, which meant that those trying the cigarette for the first time hated it.

Interestingly, RJR somehow missed the overwhelming consumer rejection of the product's taste and aroma, and pressed ahead with rollout.

The Cigarette "Experience": To smokers, smoking a cigarette is more than simply a means of ingesting nicotine, it is an experience. Many smokers enjoy the artistry of lighting a cigarette and watching the tobacco catch fire and emit smoke—which, to many smokers, holds a certain fascination. The burning cigarette also functions psychologically as a time indicator: smokers know that by the time a cigarette has been smoked and burned to its end, a certain amount of time has passed, and, for example, they know that their break is over and that it's time to get back to work.

Premier was introduced as a revolutionary "smokeless cigarette," so smokers could no longer appreciate its smoke. The cigarette couldn't be lit with a regular match or even with a regular lighter—it required the purchase of a special butane lighter which was not readily available—so smokers could not bring the cigarette "alive" in the traditional way. As for using the burn duration of a cigarette as a time indicator, it was difficult to tell when the Premier stopped burning, which was noted as a fire hazard.

Acknowledging that Premier did not come close to meeting expectations, company spokeswoman Betsy Annese said "We learned an awful lot in these test markets," adding that some "refinements" of Premier's taste and aroma were needed, as well as an improved consumer education campaign.

In my opinion, if RJR had properly and effective defined the strategic initiative and its associated tasks, the company would have known before launching the pilot test that the cigarette would have been overwhelmingly rejected by the tobacco consumer.

Premier's Target Market Demographic

Within the Premier product strategy, there is evidence to suggest that the marketing plan either failed to properly define the initiatives necessary to achieve Premier's launch goals or they neglected to adhere to them and adjust their plan as necessary based on the product testing phase of development. For instance, in support of RJR's goal for Premier *to increase its tobacco sales volume*, the organization seemed to be conflicted about the demographic of its target consumer for the product launch pilot: on the one hand, the evidence shows that RJR targeted "affluent" smokers with Premier, and on the other hand, there is evidence that RJR surreptitiously targeted young smokers.

To grow tobacco sales volume and increase its share in the U.S. market, RJR would have had to attract new users and steal existing users away from its competitors since the market for tobacco users was finite and shrinking annually by the early 1980s. The tobacco business was still enormously profitable, but the number of smokers had been in steady decline for years. RJR could have boosted its profit *only by taking market share away from others*. One additional point of market share for a premium brand can mean $450 million a year in additional sales. It would have served RJR well to define a competitive win initiative for Premier, but all indications are that none was defined.

The Premier cigarette cost about 25 percent more per pack than other cigarettes on the market, depending on state and local taxes. The higher production costs forced a higher price tag. The higher price (a 25 percent premium for cigarettes was, as it is today, very expensive) supported RJR's plan to target affluent users as its target demographic: RJR selected the initial markets with its targeted audience of older (over 25), urban smokers in mind. The Arizona cities they targeted for the pilot, in particular, were skewed toward older smokers. To attract upscale smokers, RJR positioned the smokeless cigarette as a "technological breakthrough" and used ads that were less image-oriented and more "copy-oriented" than typical cigarette ads.

While there is ample evidence that RJR targeted older tobacco users with Premier, there is overwhelming evidence that the company also targeted teenagers with the product.

"Today's teenager is tomorrow's potential regular customer, and the overwhelming majority of smokers first begin to smoke while in their teens," noted a 1981 Philip Morris corporate memo. "At least part of the success of Marlboro Red during its most rapid growth period was because it became the brand of choice among teenagers who then stuck with it as they grew older." The document defined teenagers as those 12 to 19 years old.

In 1990, RJR memos show that some RJR managers urged sales representatives to focus promotional efforts on stores close to high schools and colleges where potential young smokers would gather. The company reprimanded the managers, and in an apology letter, one of the managers explained he had been inspired with "a sense of enthusiasm with our *company's decision to gain share of market by targeting the young adult market* with numerous promotions geared toward the 'Marlboro' smoker."

The lack of a focused marketing plan designed to gain market share is a clear indication that RJR had not effectively defined focused market-capture initiatives and the associated tasks to ensure the success of either attracting existing affluent users or attracting teenagers and new young smokers into the ranks of Premier smokers, whichever group was their primary interest. *You cannot successfully accomplish both with a singular strategy.*

[2] Tasks for Satisfying U.S. Regulatory Requirements

One of the major controversies surrounding Premier was the brand's possible appeal to younger people. Here is an extract from a statement by many leading U.S. health organizations shortly after R.J. Reynolds announced the new project:

The American Cancer Society, American Heart Association, and American Lung Association have filed a petition with the U.S. Food and Drug Administration (FDA), asking that Premier be regulated as a drug. In filing this petition, we are not calling for an outright ban on Premier. We want simply for it to be properly tested before people use it.

We are especially concerned that Premier's intriguing high-tech design will lure children and teenagers into the web of nicotine addiction. RJR's marketing emphasis on 'clean enjoyment' also may lull people who already smoke into a deceptive sense of safety …

According to the FDA, any product that claims it is healthier or safer (RJR marketed Premier as "a cleaner smoke") must be FDA-regulated. In addition, the American Medical Association objected to the test marketing because the Food and Drug Administration had never concluded that Premier was not a drug. The FDA told RJR that it could market Premier at the risk of having it removed later from stores if the agency determined it was a drug that needed regulation. RJR went ahead with the market testing because they did not expect regulation.

Though RJR conducted extensive scientific research before marketing Premier, a regulatory initiative for the cigarette would have taken into account the FDA's potential classification of Premier as a drug, thus reducing—if not totally avoiding—the brand's controversy with anti-smoking advocates.

[3] Address Health Concerns in the U.S. Related to Smoking Cigarettes and Second-Hand Smoke

In a press statement, a RJR spokesman wrote in response to growing public concern about second-hand cigarette smoke: "I think we can all agree that for many non-smokers and for many smokers second-hand smoke is an annoyance, and to be able to reduce and almost eliminate that annoyance is a very positive step in the right direction." It is clear that RJR's approach to market with Premier was somewhat scattershot; there was no focused marketing effort and the brand tried to be all things to all people, which, history shows is a strategy destined to fail.

In their book, *The 21 Immutable Laws of Marketing*, Al Ries and Jack Trout discuss Pepsi-Cola's growth during the 1980s when it changed its focus to reaching the teenage market. Pepsi-Cola went from being outsold by Coca-Cola in the late 1950s by 20 percent, to being only 10 percent behind in total sales in the United States. The authors wrote, "There seems to be an almost religious belief that the wider net catches more customers, in spite of many examples to the contrary."

David Iauco, senior vice president of R.J. Reynolds, contended that the cigarette, which did not burn its tobacco content, would turn a scientific accomplishment into improved market share. Iauco expected *most smokers to remain loyal to regular cigarettes* (then who, exactly, did RJR expect market share capture to come from?), but said Premier's technology could calm growing complaints about offensive cigarette smoke and its danger to nonsmokers. "We saw a marketing opportunity to develop a cigarette with new technology that would respond to these criticisms," he said. My question is this: if there were no regulations banning smoking in public places in 1987 and 1988 due to second-hand smoke, how much of the smoking public did RJR think would care about the "new technology"? In addition, this marketing message provoked opposition from many U.S. health organizations, which also served to make potential product users skeptical.

U.S. health concerns regarding cigarette smoke in the mid-1980s were manifold and were identical to today's concerns, including: cancers, nicotine addiction, persistent cough, decreased physical performance, plaque on the artery wall, thrombosis inside a blood vessel, increased blood pressure, peptic ulcers, increased risk of having stillborn or premature infants, impotence, and gum disease, among many others. How many of these health concerns did Premier satisfactorily address per its strategic initiative to do so? The answer: none! In fact, it was found that Premier added health risks to the list, including, for instance, higher levels of some toxins.

The Premier strategic initiative *to address U.S. health*

concerns failed to deliver on the requirements of the associated objective because the tasks needed to realize the initiative were flawed in not only their definition and cause-and-effect design, but also in their adroitness. This should have been another indication—throughout the strategic initiative development process—that the initiative would ultimately be unsuccessful and that RJR would face continued public relations battles over the brand and public health concerns.

In February 1989, RJR abandoned the Premier project due to poor reception by smokers and a storm of protest from anti-smoking activists.

The Premier experience is an example of the critical nature of developing and executing fact-based initiatives within a strategic plan; because of the company's failure to properly develop the initiatives discussed above or to execute them, the Premier initiative failed. As one management educator put it, strategic planning has become more of a "check the box" exercise than a brutally frank and open confrontation of the facts; something RJR did not do.

If, on the other hand, RJR had developed its initiative-supporting tasks with candor and based on facts which provided a high degree of confidence that their execution would have resulted in the realization of the associated initiative, I contend that the Premier test market launch would have had exponentially higher odds of success.

INITIATIVES: THE KEY TO RJR'S GOAL TO INCREASE MARKET SHARE AND SALES VOLUME

Around the time of the Premier cigarette market launch, R. J. Reynolds held a 32.6 percent share of the U.S. cigarette sales market and Philip Morris held a 37.9 percent share of the $35 billion industry, according to industry reports. And since Philip Morris' market share was increasing approximately 1% annually at the time whereas RJR's had decreased or remained flat at best, it is reasonable to conclude that a quantifiable RJR objective would have been to increase U.S. market share by 1% annually (or at least by the $325 million spent on the development and launch of Premier).

So, if one of RJR's quantified objectives was to increase its domestic market share by 1%, and the critical initiative put forth to drive that share increase was Premier, then, for that leg of the strategy, it could be argued that the initiative *to develop and market Premier* was the key element of the strategy related to increased market share and volume growth. Put more simply, the *initiative* was the most important element of RJR's share capture plan, and, collectively by the same logic, the initiatives were the most important elements of RJR's overall strategy. Here's why I believe this to be the case:

In *The Practice of Management*, Peter Drucker argued that "where performance and results are such vital determinants of a company's survival, the path to those results should be *identified*, *defined* ..." Within the framework of a strategic plan, objectives are dictated by goals; if objectives are not achieved, then the goals will not be realized since objectives are the measurable indicators of the goal's successful accomplishment. A strategy's initiatives are influenced by the objectives, and they "identify" and "define" the undertakings that must be fulfilled for objectives to be realized; failure of the initiatives means failure to achieve objectives, which means goals are not accomplished which means a *failure of the strategy*. These proven relationships between the strategy elements confirm that the initiatives—above all else—are the most important elements of a strategy.

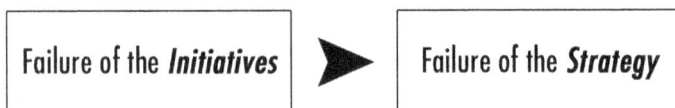

Failure of the *Initiatives*	▶	Failure of the *Strategy*

The primary reason why strategies fail is poor execution. There is evidence to suggest that improving strategy execution—both speed and quality—significantly increases the chances of a successful strategy. A key to strategic execution speed is the organization's people and how they are mobilized, supported, held accountable, and engaged in organizational strategies. Driving initiatives increases clarity and engagement by defining specific objectives and performance plans for everyone throughout the organization.

Strategy must be understood if it is to be executed and implemented, and the point where strategy gets translated into meaningful action items that define who must do what and by when in order for the strategy to be successful, is first at the initiative and then at the task level. Without well-defined initiatives, no one in the organization would know what to do to help the organization succeed by achieving its objectives and accomplishing its goals, nor would they know on what criteria their job performance is being measured. Without this, strategy implementation is not possible and it is destined for failure. As Larry Bossidy and Ram Charan wrote in their 2002 book *Execution: The Discipline of Getting Things Done*: "businesses don't fail for lack of good ideas; they fail for lack of ability to implement them."

MBO AND MBI:
DIFFERENCES AND ALIGNMENT

• • •

My Management by Initiatives (MBI) proposal almost certainly raises the question: What is the difference between Drucker's Management by Objectives (MBO) and my MBI?

The concept of Management by Objectives (MBO) —and objectives as they relate to managing a business, in general—was proposed by Peter Drucker in his seminal book *The Practice of Management*. Drucker argued that "Setting objectives enables a business to get where it should be going rather than be the plaything of weather, winds and accidents. A business must be managed by setting objectives for it. To manage a business means, therefore, to manage by objectives." He also made the case that "Objectives are needed in every area where performance and results directly and vitally affect the survival and prosperity of the business."

My MBI proposition is 100 percent aligned with MBO. However, where the proposals differ is in the opinions of where the manager's (or business-unit leader's) attention and work effort should be focused. In the end, both models stress the importance of achieving business objectives since they determine goal satisfaction which drives strategy. However, objectives are not actionable; they do not define how they are to be achieved. Management by Initiatives advances the idea that the clear path to *achieving* objectives should be "identified" and "defined" as *initiatives*, and that the manager's efforts should be focused on realizing initiatives—the actionable path to *achieving* objectives—because, by successfully executing initiatives, the manager will have, in turn, achieved the objectives to which said initiatives are tied.

In this sense, MBO and MBI ultimately have the same interest: achieving objectives. However, the difference between the two is nuanced: MBO suggests managing to the objectives on which the manager's performance will be measured, whereas MBI suggests managing to the initiatives that will result in achievement of the objectives on which the manager's performance will be measured. Management by Initiatives takes Management by Objectives a step further toward action.

MBO vs. MBI

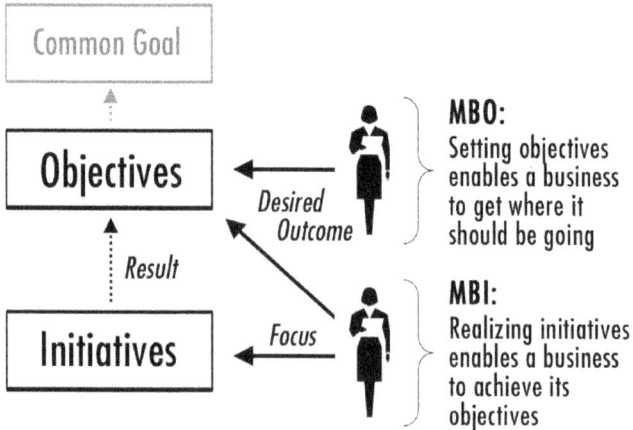

Management by Objectives provides a time-tested prescription for ensuring leaders' focus on the things that, if achieved, will drive performance and organizational success, but it does not prescribe how to achieve them. Management by Initiatives is the prescription. The similarities, nuanced differences, and alignment points are summarized below.

MBO	MBI
A business must be managed by setting objectives for it.	Objectives are critical, for they determine the successful accomplishment of the goals by which an organization is guided.
Each manager needs clearly spelled out objectives. These objectives should always derive from the business enterprise's goals.	Each manager's performance should be driven by objectives, and their *focus* should be on realizing the initiatives that achieve objectives.
Setting objectives enables a business to get where it should be going	Realizing initiatives enables an organization to achieve objectives.
Managing requires judgment; all that can be done is to make judgment possible by narrowing its range and the available alternatives, giving it clear focus, a sound foundation in facts and reliable measurement of the effects and validity of actions and decisions. And this, by the very nature of business enterprise, requires multiple objectives.	MBI also agrees with "narrowing [the] range [of judgments] and the available alternatives, giving it clear focus, a sound foundation in facts and *reliable measurement of the effects and validity of actions* and decisions."
Objectives are needed in every area where performance and results directly and vitally affect the business' survival and prosperity.	Initiatives are needed in every area where objectives are pursued if the objectives are to have any chance of being achieved.
How to set objectives: by determining what shall be measured in each area and what the measurement yardstick should be. For the utilized measurement determines what one pays attention to.	Objectives cannot be achieved without the pursuit and execution of initiatives. The successful realization of initiatives is what managers should focus on.
Each member of the enterprise contributes something different, but they must all contribute toward a common goal.	The focus on actionable initiatives—which support objectives which in turn support goals—and the tasks necessary to realize the initiatives, drive alignment at all organization levels and focuses everyone's efforts on a common goal.

An example of how MBO and MBI ultimately have the same aim (the achievement of objectives) and how MBI takes MBO a step further can be seen below.

Drucker argues that: "The objective of the district sales manager's job should be defined by the contribution he and his district sales force have to make to the sales department." I agree. The sales manager's performance should be based on his or her achievement of goals and objectives that define the manager's contribution to the organization.

The sales manager's job is more than delivering numerical metrics such as sales revenue and attaining quotas; a significant part of the sales manager job is performing non-numeric activities and accomplishing often-subjective goals (which could be converted to measurable objectives), such as training, coaching, and developing sales representatives, and building strong client and partner coalitions, for instance. These activities are also "contributions" to the sales manager's organization. However the sales manager's job is defined, one thing is clear: the sales manager must *do something* to achieve his or her objectives and accomplish their goals.

In my many years of experience in sales, sales leadership, and sales consulting working with sales managers, executives, and professionals around the world on upgrading sales performance, I have found one thing to be universally true: it is the sales *initiatives* that define how the sales manager will deliver what Drucker called the "contribution he and his district sales force have to make to the sales department"—the objectives.

Some time ago while leading a multi-billion dollar sales organization, I was concerned about the organization's stagnant sales performance, as indicated by sales dollars as a percentage of the goal. I analyzed the sales processes in place at the time, the sales margins we were generating on various deals, clients gained, lost, and the rate of customer churn, and the way the sales teams were measures for their performance reviews.

My analysis revealed something that helped me understand my organization's performance at the time I took over the leadership role: (1) there was no alignment between the corporation's business-unit-level strategy and the activities of the sales managers or the sales teams; (2) there was no definable connection between the sales team's quota objectives and their daily activities; and (3) there was no correlation between the sales discounts the managers gave to clients and clients' commitment to the company; clients that were given steep discounts were just as likely to defect as clients that had received less-favorable pricing from us.

From the MBO standpoint, sales managers were given measurable sales objectives which they worked to achieve. Unfortunately, the sales managers were not assigned objectives related to client retention and sales margin. From the MBI standpoint, however, the sales managers' activities were not guided by initiatives that would have led to the achievement of their sales objectives. As a result, managers engaged in many unfocused activities that had no bearing on achieving their sales objectives and performance suffered.

In time, after initiating specific sales strategies with distinct initiatives designed to achieve sales objectives, the sales managers' performance improved and overall sales as a percent to goal improved significantly, in addition to other performance improvement gains.

SEVEN

TOWARD MANAGEMENT
BY INITIATIVES

• • •

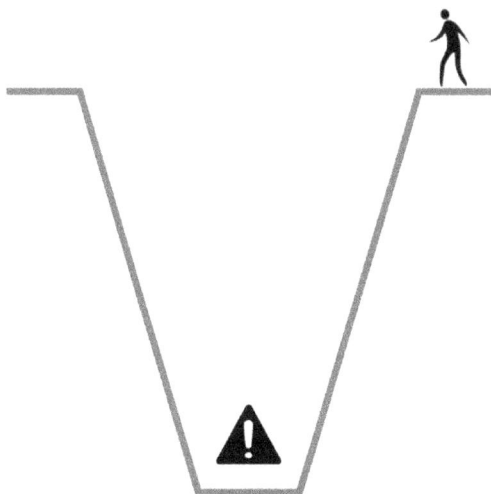

CROSSING THE RAVINE

Assume you are stranded at the edge of a high cliff surrounding a huge, deep ravine with strong currents, and you need to make it to the other side of the ravine because a dangerous storm is approaching. Laying on the ground at cliff's edge were four pamphlets: the first pamphlet explained the reason why you needed to get to the other side of the ravine and its importance to your survival; the second pamphlet described how you would know that you have safely arrived at the other side of the ravine; a third pamphlet described the Mac-Gyver-esque project you needed to complete to safely get to the other side of the ravine; and the fourth pamphlet described the step-by-step instructions of how to complete the MacGyver-esque project.

While standing at the edge of the cliff, you see a multi-span bridge without a railing, and a sign that reads: "Elevated trail tread and causeway to the other side of the ravine is located 18 miles northeast. Approximate time to the destination is 10 hours"; and a cable with some "straps" wrapped around the base of a tree. Seeing these things you realize there are several potential options for crossing the ravine—and, being a good swimmer, you even contemplate the long-shot possibility of swimming across—but, you don't know which method will get you across safely and with enough time to spare before the storm hits.

To determine your path forward, you pick up the

pamphlets and start to read them.

Pamphlet #1: "You must cross the ravine to avoid being harmed by the dangerous approaching storm, and to safely continue on your journey home."

Pamphlet #2: "You will know that you have successfully and safely crossed the ravine when both of your feet firmly stand on the ground at least 50 feet away from the edge of the opposite cliff. You must also reach the other side of the ravine within 30 minutes, which is when the storm is expected to hit."

Pamphlet #3: "There are many options available to you for crossing the ravine, but the option that is safest and has the best odds of getting you to the other side of the ravine securely within 30 minutes is to use the cable and harness ('straps') to create a one-rope bridge. Swimming is suicidal due to the strong currents; the rickety bridge is not secure and is likely to collapse; and it will take you 10 hours to hike to the causeway."

Pamphlet #4: "The steps necessary to use the cable and harness to create a one-rope bridge and the instructions for how to use the cable to Tyrol across the ravine are detailed in this pamphlet. First, use the cable to tie a fixed-loop knot to the tree, then secure it to the tree using a transport knot. When the line is secured, put on the harness, clip it onto the cable, and use the Rappel Seat Method to make your way across the ravine …"

All of the pamphlets are necessary for your survival in light of the pending storm: Pamphlet #1 advises that you must get to the other side of the ravine for your safety; Pamphlet #2 tells you specifically how you will know that you are safe; Pamphlet #3 tells you how to get to safety; and Pamphlet #4 provides the instructions for doing so. But, one of the pamphlets holds the key to your survival; it provides the only way to get to the other side safely, and that is *Pamphlet #3*.

Whether stranded on the edge of a dangerous ravine or lost in the wilderness, the only—and most important—thing you want to know is "*How* do I get back to safety?" At that point, you already know that your survival depends on you getting out of there safely (Pamphlet #1, your *goal*), and you know that you must travel some distance and do so quickly before your food runs out or you cross paths with a bear (Pamphlet #2, your *objective*). But, the way to get out of your predicament and back to safety, an answer to your "How" question, is the most important to your survival (Pamphlet #3). In this example, Pamphlet #3 is the strategy *initiative*.

Sometimes, when I am speaking to a group of business leaders and the discussion topic is the importance of strategic initiatives in successful strategy execution, someone suggests that the *tasks* are more important than the initiatives, because the tasks prescribe the specific things that must be done to realize the initiative. They argue that without the tasks nothing gets done, not even the initiatives, and, therefore, the strategy dies.

I agree that a strategy cannot be executed if no tasks are performed toward that end. The challenge with this argument of the tasks being the most important strategy elements is that *tasks do not exist without the initiatives which dictate their existence.* Tasks are subordinate actions to the initiative and are, therefore, dependent on the initiative for direction; they cannot stand alone nor can they occur independently of the associated initiative. Because tasks require the dictates of initiatives for their existence, they cannot be considered more important than that which determines their definition and, more importantly, their value.

I liken it to a computer system and its programmers. In 2011, IBM's Watson computer astonished everyone when it won a Jeopardy match against two human contestants, thus becoming known as "the world's smartest computer." But, how smart or useful is Watson without the human developers and programmers that dictate what Watson does and how it does it? In this equation, the human programmers (and developers, servicers, and parts manufacturers …) are more critical to successful problem resolution than is Watson. To be certain, Watson alone as a resource is quite important and significant, but its significance and ability to impact an outcome—execute—are dependent on and determined by another entity. Having spent more than 25 years in the technology sector, my argument is that the human element is more important to executing a plan than the computer the human beings control.

Another way to look at it is thusly: You have been hired to bake a very beautiful and very complex "Enchanted Forest" wedding cake for the Royal Wedding.

You have never baked this cake before, but you have been given a great step-by-step recipe by none other than the chef Rosalind Miller, voted Best Wedding Cake Designer at the 2012 Wedding Industry Awards.

When you arrive at the Royal kitchen, you reach into your bag and pull out the wedding cake recipe: "Strawberry Vanilla Cheesecake!" This, too, is a top-10-voted wedding cake recipe, but it's not the Enchanted Forest recipe, so how valuable is the Strawberry Vanilla Cheesecake recipe to you at that moment? Not very useful at all. In this example, *to bake an Enchanted Forest cake* is the initiative, and the step-by-step recipe instructions are the tasks necessary to bake the cake. The Strawberry Vanilla Cheesecake recipe—while award-winning—is useless to you based on the initiative that you are trying to accomplish. The point is this: tasks, like the Strawberry Vanilla Cheesecake recipe, can be very valuable and necessary to execute a strategy. However, their value is determined by the initiative which they support, otherwise, tasks are useless toward executing a strategy; their importance rests at the feet of initiatives.

An argument can also be made that, by this same logic, strategy objectives are more important to the strategy's execution than the initiatives, because objectives dictate initiatives. The problem with this position is that objectives, unlike initiatives, are *not* actionable. Execution is about doing things; it is about undertaking action to achieve objectives.

The strength of a strategy lies in the elements that

not only define what the organization must do toward accomplishing its goals, but also how it must be done. This is the essence of execution. Within a strategy, there is only one element where this is the case: the initiatives.

INITIATIVES IN ACTION

A Starbucks on Every Corner

In the early 2000s, Starbucks was riding a wave of success and had started to expand locations to more states and countries. At one point, it was so bad that, while on a business trip in Manhattan, I saw there were Starbucks coffee shops directly across the street from one another on multiple streets and nearly every block. I remember thinking: does every block need two Starbucks?

By 2008, the over-expansion diluted profits and net income had fallen significantly, cutting the stock price in half. To turn around the company's fortunes, Starbucks CEO Howard Schultz defined three initiatives that yielded positive results.

1. Shut down under-performing stores. Starbucks shuttered nearly 1,000 under-performing stores, cutting salaries and real estate leasing costs.

2. Improve the product. That year, Starbucks closed all 7,000 U.S. stores for three hours to retrain baristas on how to make a good cup of espresso; Starbucks also did away with automatic espresso machines. Good move!

3. Make the stores more welcoming. Starbucks began to encourage customers to spend time in their stores, and to help the process, they made free Wi-Fi available in all stores in 2010.

The initiatives paid off, and Starbucks experienced a solid turnaround. While the goal (improve shareholder wealth) and the objectives (reduce costs, increase sales) were necessary targets, it was through the successful execution of these types of initiatives that the Starbucks turnaround was a success.

The New Old Spice Guy

The Old Spice aftershave brand needed an overhaul. For years, the brand represented "your dad's" cinnamon-smelling aftershave, and it fell within the middle of its category. Procter & Gamble implemented a strategy to appeal to a younger demographic and jump-start the brand, so, in 2007, the company and its agency, Wieden + Kennedy, launched the first in a series of brand-image-changing spots. The first one featured actor Bruce Campbell babbling about "If you have it, you don't need it ..." The spot was a hit, and it was followed up in 2010 with the ad that arguably propelled the brand into the consciousness of a new demographic: Isaiah Mustafa, as the viral sensation "Old Spice Guy."

P&G's goal for Old Spice was to improve its sales and propel it to the top of its category, following an initiative to improve the brand's image for a younger demographic.

BECOMING OPERATIONAL:
A PROCESS FOR DEFINING INITIATIVES

In complex organizations, business-unit leaders, functional leaders, and managers—*distributed leaders*—are responsible for strategy execution. They are the doers, and the success or failure of a strategy rests with them. So, while these managers are responsible for executing strategy, senior leadership must take responsibility for not only guiding an organization's strategic execution, but also supporting distributed leaders in their execution efforts by providing resources, guidance, and support.

An organization's executives must, therefore, think operationally if they are to provide the necessary guidance and support to enable a strategy's execution. Strategy is about what to do and operations is about doing it. Deming wrote that an organization is a system, an interdependent group of items, people, and processes with a common purpose: *to achieve results*. Within the framework of a strategy, *results* are achieved by realizing initiatives, by acting operationally. Following this train of thought, it can be argued that the common purpose of the system—the organization—is to accomplish initiatives.

But, how does a manager think more operationally and go about defining aligned, results-yielding initiatives within the strategic planning process? A proven best practice toward that end is threefold: define the differences between the organization's current state and its desired state; perform internal and external strategic analysis; and answer the three critical MBI initiative-development questions.

Difference Reduction

Improvement is based on a reduction in variation, whether that means variation between the specifications and quality of output in the manufacturing process or a reduction in the differences between where you are today and where you want to be at some point in the future.

The difference-reduction method of problem solving and initiative & task development involves understanding where you are today, determining where you want to be at some point in the future, and identifying the differences and similarities between the two states. Once this is accomplished, an organization can then put plans in place to resolve the differences between the two states (i.e., define initiatives), until it has reached its desired state. This, of course, implies the need for a way to evaluate the differences between the two states.

Here is a simple example. If the Acme Computer Company wanted to increase its client access, grow revenue, and save money by joining the Microsoft Partner Network and becoming a Microsoft Partner, the company would identify the potential differences between their status as a Microsoft Partner and the company as it stands today. These differences will provide a list of potential tasks and initiatives that must be realized for Acme Computer Company to accomplish its goal of becoming a Microsoft partner.

Microsoft membership opportunities have an individual set of core requirements, and for each opportunity, Acme must fulfill the minimum requirements (below).

Acme Computer Company Today	Difference	Acme as a Microsoft Partner
Not accomplished	Paid membership fee (annual investment): **task**	Paid membership fees.
Not accomplished	Complete a partner profile: **task**	Completed partner profile
Not accomplished	Customer references: **task**	Provided customer references
Not accomplished	Business-focused competency assessments (meet a minimum Microsoft-related revenue commitment): **initiative** (if not met today)	Met the minimum Microsoft-related revenue commitment
Not accomplished	Technical credentials: Technology professionals must pass the technical exam and/or assessment: **initiative**	Passed the technical exam and assessment

Even though *joining the Microsoft Partner Network* can be an initiative itself, this simplistic example is provided to illustrate how the process of difference reduction can identify additional potential initiatives and tasks that may be overlooked.

For Acme, these five requirements were the difference between the company's current state (as a suboptimal performer) and its desired state (to become a Microsoft partner). For Acme to become a Microsoft Partner, it would have to eliminate the differences between its current state and its desired state—hence, the term "difference-reduction." For each difference that Acme eliminates, the total number of differences is reduced until all differences have been eliminated, leaving no difference between Acme and "Acme the Microsoft Partner": the desired state.

Three Manage by Initiatives Planning Questions for Defining Initiatives to Support an Objective

After a strategy's goals and objectives have been developed ensuring a cause-and-effect relationship between them, the next stage in the planning process is to define the initiatives that lead to and support objective achievement.

The process of defining initiatives can be as simple as answering three fundamental questions:

1. **What are all of the "things" that must be done to deliver the quantifiable metrics defined in the objective?** [Develop a complete list of the potential projects or initiatives (not specific action items or *tasks*) that would lead to objective satisfaction].

2. **If we successfully accomplish each of these "things" (initiatives, projects), are we at least 95% confident that we will, as a result, achieve the quantifiable metrics defined in the objective?** [Before proceeding, the answer must be "Yes"].

3. **How do we *know* that the successful accomplishment of each of the initiatives/projects will result in successful objective achievement?** [This question relates to the cause-and-effect nature of the objective-initiative relationship of the strategy].

Example: Voluntary Employee Attrition

Frequent voluntary turnover has a negative impact on employee morale, productivity, and an organization's revenue. Plus, recruiting and training a new employee requires time and money, sometimes as much as sixty percent more money than the cost of retaining an existing employee.

The Center for American Progress reports that for workers earning less than $50,000 annually—which covers three-quarters of all workers in the United States—the typical cost of turnover is 20 percent of the employee's salary. So, if a departing employee had an annual salary of $50,000, the cost to replace that employee would be approximately $10,000. Multiply that number by the number of employees who voluntarily leave an organization each year (a 2013 CompData Surveys report found the average voluntary employee turnover rate in all industries in the U.S. was 10.4 percent), and you can gain an appreciation for the importance of employee retention.

If the Acme Computer Company established a goal *to improve employee morale and reduce voluntary employee attrition,* and an attrition objective was *to reduce its current voluntary attrition rate from 7 percent to 4 percent next year*—saving the 10,000 person company nearly $1.2 million—the company might answer the three MBI planning questions related to this objective as follows:

1. **What are all of the "things" that must be done to deliver the quantifiable metrics defined in the objective to** *"reduce its current voluntary attrition rate from 7 percent to 4 percent next year"*?

   Acme's Human Resources team defined a series of potential initiatives that could support its attrition-reduction objective.

- Engage employees and show the connection between their work and the organization's goals;
- Foster a sense of workplace community;
- Foster employee development;
- Create a high-feedback environment and make sure employees know what is expected of them;
- Offer a competitive benefits package that fits the employees' needs and provides different benefits to different employees;

- Implement an incentive & rewards program to help keep workers motivated and feeling rewarded;

- Foster open communication. Conduct "stay" and "exit" interviews.

2. **If we successfully accomplish each of these "things" (initiatives, projects), are we at least 95% confident that we will, as a result, achieve the quantifiable metrics defined in the objective?**

Acme's Potential Initiatives	Confidence in Achieving the Objective
Engage employees and show the connection between their work and the organization's goals	Low-Medium
Foster a sense of workplace community	High
Foster employee development	High
Create a high-feedback environment and make sure employees know what is expected of them	High
Offer a competitive benefits package that fits the employees' needs and provides different benefits for different employees	High
Implement an incentive & rewards program to help keep workers motivated and feeling rewarded	Medium
Foster open communication. Conduct "stay" and "exit" interviews.	Low-Medium

Yes. The Acme Human Resources team is confident that, collectively, these initiatives will reduce voluntary attrition by more than the three percent target objective.

3. **How do we *know* that the successful accomplishment of each of the initiatives/projects will result in successful object achievement?**

The initiatives listed above have been time-tested and proven to create "effective commitment" to the organization, because they increase employees' emotional connection to the organization and their fellow associates and work group. The positive effect (of realizing these initiatives) on turnover has been demonstrated by empirical studies. In other words, these initiatives have been proven to result in (cause) a decrease in voluntary employee attrition (effect).

Internal and External Analysis

It is pretty common for organizations to carry out planning by performing internal and external analyses of forces that affect an organization's performance. External analysis is critical to evaluating a company's competitive positioning and is, therefore, valuable in formulating a business-unit-level strategy designed to provide a sustainable competitive advantage. The external analysis will inform the company on the *threats* it has to mitigate and the *opportunities* that are available to exploit. The internal analysis informs an organization on its *strengths* it must leverage and the *weaknesses* that inhibit performance and must, therefore, be addressed. The most common environmental analysis that organizations perform to support their strategic planning efforts is the Strengths-Weaknesses-Opportunities-Threats or "SWOT" analysis.

SWOT analysis requires an organization to thoroughly analyze a single (at a time) aspect of itself (such as a product, investment opportunity, or the organization's market position), gain a better perspective of its position, and make decisions based on where the organization believes it has competitive advantages, has weaknesses, is vulnerable, and where it should look for new opportunities. The environmental and SWOT analyses give the organization an indication of the issues on which they should focus and prioritize; this prioritization will help guide the goal-setting activities associated with the organization's strategy, and define the initiatives required to address any identified issues and exploit available opportunities. This is illustrated in the diagram below.

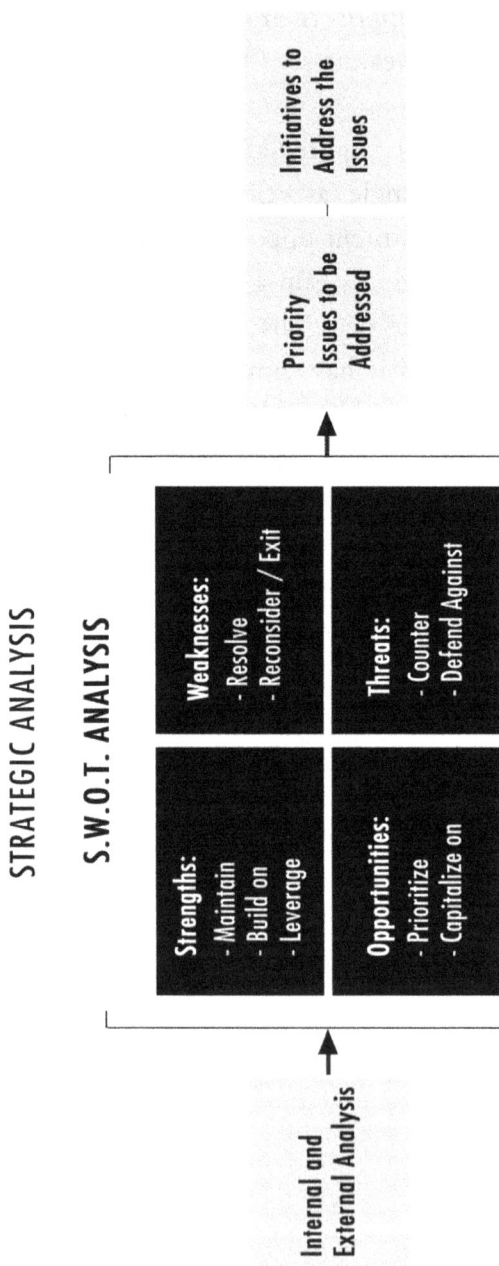

STRATEGIC ANALYSIS

S.W.O.T. ANALYSIS

Strengths:
- Maintain
- Build on
- Leverage

Weaknesses:
- Resolve
- Reconsider / Exit

Opportunities:
- Prioritize
- Capitalize on

Threats:
- Counter
- Defend Against

Internal and External Analysis

Priority Issues to be Addressed

Initiatives to Address the Issues

The goal of this type of strategic analysis is to identify those things that will help or hinder the organization's ability to achieve its vision, and to ensure that the strategy it develops leverages the organization's strengths, pursues the identified opportunities, addresses its competitive weaknesses, and counters/defends against conditions that threaten its competitive position.

If done effectively, this form of strategic analysis will yield a list of priority issues that a strategy must address, and a list of potential initiatives needed to address the issues.

In my experience working with organizations and business leaders on the development and execution of business-unit-level strategies, I have found that engaging in the aforementioned environmental analysis, the process of difference reduction, and answering the three MBI planning questions is an easy-yet-effective way to define a brainstormed list of potential initiatives designed to achieve an associated objective. Whichever approach is used to develop a list of potential initiatives, however, the most important things to consider are to:

- Ensure a cause-and-effect relationship exists between potential initiatives and their associated objective;

- Use experience, historical data, and other available research to gain confidence that the potential initiatives in which your organization may engage will contribute to and/or result in the achievement of the associated objective;

- Answer the improvement questions below not only for typical strategy elements—the goals and objectives—but also for the potential initiatives:
  - » What are we trying to accomplish?
  - » What's broken and how do we know it's broken?
  - » What do we want to change (do differently)?
  - » How will we know that a change is an improvement?
  - » What changes can we make that will result in an improvement?

These best practices will give you the greatest chance of crafting initiatives that, if successfully executed, have the highest likelihood of leading to the successful achievement of their associated objectives.

LINKING MANAGEMENT BY INITIATIVES AND ASSOCIATES' PERFORMANCE PLANS

In the previous example of Acme Computer Company's goal of reducing voluntary employee attrition, I referenced the importance of creating a high-feedback environment to make sure employees know what is expected of them, and engaging employees to show the connection between their work and the organization's goals.

This Acme example introduces the importance of linking associates' expected performance (as defined in their performance plans) and organizational goals. An organization's associates are more engaged and productive when they know what is expected of them and have a clear understanding of how their role in the organization contributes to the organization's performance (as measured by goal achievement). And, as I have made the case throughout, the greatest impact business-unit leaders, functional leaders, managers, and work-unit-level associates can have on the organization's goals and objectives is the successful realization of its initiatives and the execution of the tasks needed to do so.

If a strategy is to be given the best chance of succeeding, organizations must develop an approach for cascading goals all the way down to the work-unit level. This is most effectively done through initiatives and, to a degree, associated tasks. At the work-unit level (and relevant to their role in the organization), associates should be measured on their accomplishments that directly affect the organization's goals and objectives. And their accomplishments in this regard should be the successful realization of initiatives based on the tasks (which have defined completion timeframes and can contain measurable values) that are required to do so (depending on the associate's role in the organization).

Goal-Performance Plan Alignment

When *managing* by initiatives, it is essential to *measure by initiatives*. To do otherwise is, for instance, akin to managing a department to the amount of revenue it generates, and not measuring associates' performance based on the revenue the department generates; there is an unproductive and de-motivating disconnect between expected results and job expectations. The more emphasis an organization can place on each associate's ability to execute their assignments (tasks, initiatives, etc.) and their success at doing so, the greater the organization's outcomes. And the most effective way of emphasizing the importance of executing assignments and its relationship to associate's job performance rating is by building execution metrics and activities into performance plans.

A strategy's initiatives are the point in strategy where the organization's vision and desires become real to the people in the organization responsible for executing the strategy. Basing associates' performance on the execution of clearly-defined initiatives and tasks, the associates' job expectations and performance-measurement criteria become easier to understand, less ambiguous, and more fair to them. This increases associate engagement and motivation which, studies show, can improve strategic execution and ultimately lead to overall greater organizational performance.

CONCLUSION

. . .

While writing the manuscript for this book, I happened to be half-watching a sports news channel during the start of the (American) football season. What caught my attention were the many times various National Football League (NFL) coaches said, "Our goal is to win our division." I almost expected some team owner to storm down to the podium where these coaches were being interviewed about the upcoming season, grab the microphone, and say, "Actually, the coach misspoke: Our goal this year is to win the *Super Bowl*."

The goal of every NFL team every year is to win the championship—the Super Bowl. If you asked all 32 NFL head coaches what would be their wish for the season, every one of them would say it would be to win the Super Bowl, *not* to win the division.

I suspect that after NFL coaches have had a chance to read this book, they would develop a high-level strategy for their team that might look something like this:

- **Goal**: To win the Super Bowl; …

- **Objectives**: To win 19 games this year (16 regular season games to go undefeated, 2 playoff games, and the Super Bowl; …

- **Initiatives**: Build the #1 defense in the league; build the #1 offense in the league; optimize the playbook; win the division championship to ensure a playoff spot; win a minimum of 11 games to ensure a playoff spot; win the conference championship; defeat the opposing conference champion; …

- **Tasks**: Draft and acquire players; release players; call the right plays based on in-game situations; execute the game plans perfectly; study game film; put the players in position to succeed; and fire the coach; …

If the coaches did, indeed, read this book or gain an appreciation for this form of strategy by any other means, they would come to appreciate that the most important elements of their strategy designed to win the Super Bowl are initiatives. They would come to this realization when they consider that, without getting into the playoffs (an initiative), they have a *zero* percent chance of accomplishing their goal of winning the Super Bowl.

Strategic planning should address three key questions: *What* do we do, *why* should we do it, and *how* do we do it; the third question is key because it relates to *execution.* It's one thing to determine that it is in a football team's best interest to win the Super Bowl. It's far more important to execute the action plan necessary to do it. And when it comes to execution, the initiatives ("ensuring a playoff spot") are the most important aspects.

Organization leaders must come to grips with the idea that driving initiatives as a means of achieving objectives is critical. Far too many senior leaders feel their job is done once they've defined the organization's vision and a high-level strategy outline. The evidence is clear that the most successful organizations during times of change and uncertainty (which is when leadership becomes most important) are those that focus their energies on providing detailed initiatives or projects that support the strategy, supporting the realization of the initiatives, and moving them forward.

What is of equal importance toward strategy execution is the engagement of people who have the responsibility for performing tasks that lead to realized initiatives. Execution is the most important aspect of a strategy and *people* are responsible for its execution, the speed at which execution occurs, and its quality. An organization's people, therefore, must have a clear understanding of "Why am I doing this job, what's the point?", and they must also have a clear understanding of the expectations of them toward the success of the organization's strategy; their performance measurement must be aligned with the work they are expected to perform. Unfortunately, in many organizations I have worked with, strategies are seldom translated down to the work-unit-level and the work assignments required to ensure strategy success are rarely incorporated into individual associates' performance plans.

THIS IS NOT INTENDED TO BE A "HOW-TO" BOOK about strategy development. It is, however, a book about a different way of thinking about successful strategy execution. I agree that business-unit leaders and managers should manage by objectives, but I strongly believe that for an organization to give itself the best chance of successfully executing the action plan of a strategy—and thereby, the strategy itself—its managers must *manage by initiatives*.

This book formalizes the model for managing by initiatives, and documents the rationale for the MBI proposition. But, the idea is not new. In fact, it can be traced as far back as the First Peloponnesian War (c. 460-446 BCE).

Ancient historian Thucydides chronicled nearly 30 years of war and tension between Athens and Sparta in his "History of the Peloponnesian War." In the 5th century BCE, Sparta and Athens were the two major Greek powers, and it was inevitable that their spheres of influence would overlap and cause conflict. Sparta had been particularly alarmed at the growing power of Athens and its massive fleet of ships. Sparta was most powerful as a land force, and it was the Spartans' fear of Athens, Thucydides argues, that led them to make their first, preemptive attack in 430 BCE.

The two sides approached the war from different perspectives: the Spartans understood the need to match Athenian naval strength (which they feared most), and Athens employed a strategy of exhaustion—to force Sparta to surrender by draining their economic resources. To execute their respective strategies, Sparta executed an initiative to destroy Athens by beating it at its strength: its naval fleet. With support from Persia and others, Sparta was able to match Athenian naval strength and successfully pursue their strategy of annihilation.

An examination of the strategies and initiatives employed by both sides in the war reveals that the Athenian initiatives designed to win the war were rational, yet poorly executed, leading to a failed strategy and ultimately defeat. In executing its major initiative to deplete Sparta economically, Athens failed to consider the economic support Sparta would receive from allies. This oversight resulted in a failed Athenian strategy to gain the surrender or destruction of Sparta.

Sparta, on the other hand, successfully executed the major initiatives it defined to support its grand strategy. Sparta defined initiatives to (1) capture land around Athens, (2) to destroy its crops and food supply, and (3) to build a stronger naval fleet (to deliver on its strategy to win a naval battle against Athens). Unlike the Athenians, the Spartans successfully executed its major initiatives, resulting in the successful accomplishment of its goals: to defeat Athens in a naval battle and achieve their surrender or destruction.

Many strategic thinkers, consultants, and educators have looked to the distant past for evidence of the early use of strategic planning and execution in hopes of shedding light on ways to help organizations upgrade performance, provide value, and gain competitive advantage. The frequent reference to Sun Tzu's *The Art of War* is a clear indication of this.

The majority of strategic wisdom is centered around defining an organization's mission, vision, and values. It is focused on defining the organization's goals that support its mission, vision, and values. It is, to a lesser degree, concerned with defining measurable objectives that demonstrate the accomplishment of the organization's goals. And, until now, little to no focus has been placed on what I have found to be the most important aspect of turning mission, vision, values, goals, and objectives into reality: strategic initiatives.

While Management by Initiatives (MBI) may be a new strategic planning paradigm, the idea itself is not new; as I have described above, the focus on initiatives toward a successful strategy outcome can be found as far back as that of the Spartan admiral Lysander who successfully executed Sparta's sea attack to defeat Athens' naval fleet and win the Peloponnesian War.

Strategic planning is often a time-consuming, expensive activity that consumes valuable organizational resources, including its leadership's time. Far too many of the strategies that I have reviewed over the years stop at the objective definition stage and get filed away in someone's desk drawer, only to be retrieved when a new administration is put in charge. These strategies are never effectively executed, resulting in wasted time, effort, money, and, most importantly, a missed opportunity for the organization to generate value and gain a sustainable competitive advantage—the reasons why the strategy was developed in the first place.

To quote Drucker: "To manage a business means, therefore, to manage by objectives." My position is this: To manage by objectives means to manage by initiatives. Therefore, to manage a business means to **manage by initiatives.**

ABOUT THE AUTHOR

TAB EDWARDS is a principal with The Water Group, a business services consultancy that works with business and organization leaders to help them make better, more informed decisions, convert those decisions into actions, and deliver sustainable success. His principles have been adopted by organizations around the world, and his best practices implemented by firms of every type, including: global enterprises, corporations, SMBs, start-ups, public sector organizations, universities, and non-profits.

Edwards is the author of ten books, including an Amazon.com Bestseller, and is a globally recognized consultant and critical thinker with expertise in business-unit level strategy and execution.

Prior to The Water Group, Edwards has held global consulting and leadership positions at some of the world's most admired companies, including: IBM Corporation, General Electric, AmerisourceBergen, and Hewlett-Packard.

To learn more about The Water Group and The Water Performance Academy, please visit www.Water215.com.

THE WATER PERFORMANCE ACADEMY

SPEAKING ENGAGEMENTS AND STRATEGY WORKSHOPS

Tab Edwards and the professionals at The Water Performance Academy are available to work with leaders and organizations of every stripe in various capacities, including:

SPEAKING ENGAGEMENTS

Whether inspiring audiences, motivating teams, or delivering keynote addresses, we are prepared to deliver an engagement that will motivate your team to higher performance levels and provide them with useful information, while doing so in an entertaining and uplifting manner.

COACHING WORKSHOPS

Our professionals have worked with organization leaders, managers, and individual contributors globally on becoming more effective in their given areas of responsibility, and upgrading their overall performance and effectiveness across various functional areas, including: sales, management, team development, strategy and strategy execution, and communication to name a few.

BUSINESS PROCESS IMPROVEMENT
WORKSHOPS

By providing organizations with a clear benchmark of their current state performance and the issues impeding progress and goal-attainment, we work with organizations to identify areas of inefficiency, underperformance, and high cost, and to define improvement solutions.

STRATEGY WORKSHOPS

The Water Performance Academy's team can work with your organization on every aspect of the business-unit level strategy, including planning sessions, workgroup discussions, current-strategy analysis, strategy development workshops, strategy scorecarding, strategy execution engagement, and strategy coaching & guidance.

THE WATER PERFORMANCE ACADEMY
AN ENTITY OF THE WATER GROUP, LLC
WATER215.COM

• • •

We don't do everything, but what we do,
we do quite well:

Business-Unit Strategy & Strategic Planning
Sales Assessment & Optimization
Business Process Improvement
MPS

• • •

Working with organizations to make informed decisions,
convert those decisions to actions, and deliver sustainable success;
since 1993

SELECTED BIBLIOGRAPHY

"2014 Surgeon General's Report: The Health Consequences of Smoking—50 Years of Progress." Centers for Disease Control and Prevention, 26 Feb. 2015

"Achievements in Public Health, 1900-1999: Tobacco Use -- United States, 1900-1999"; Centers for Disease Control and Prevention; <http://www.cdc.gov/mmwr/preview/mmwrhtml/mm4843a2.htm>.

Ansoff, H. Igor. *Strategic Management*. New York: Wiley, 1979.

Ansoff, H. I. "The Emerging Paradigm of Strategic Behavior." *Strategic Management Journal*, Vol. 8, 501-515. 1987

Ansoff, H. I., Declerck, R. P. & Hayes, R. L. *From Strategic Planning to Strategic Management*. John Wiley, New York. 1976.

Arman, R. "Fragmentation and power in managerial work in health care. A study of first and second line-managers." University of Gothenburg. School of Business, Economics and Law. August 2010.

Arman, R. "What Do Managers Really Do at Work." Göteborgs Universitet. October 2010. <http://handels.gu.se/english/about-the-School/visiting-professor-programme/news/news-detail//what-do-managers-really-do-at-work.cid958106>.

"The Art and Science of Measuring CEO Performance." *Knowledge@Wharton.* The Wharton School, University of Pennsylvania, 22 August, 2007. Web. 06 April, 2015 <http://knowledge.wharton.upenn.edu/article/the-art-and-science-of-measuring-ceo-performance/>

Bauman, Jennifer. «Kauai›s Wild Chickens: The Good, the Bad, and the Ugly!» *Kauai Blog.* 11 Mar. 2013. <https://kauaiblog.wordpress.com/2013/03/12/kauais-wild-chickens-the-good-the-bad-and-the-ugly/>

Bartholomew, K., and Manion, J. "Community in the Workplace: A Proven Retention Strategy." *Journal of Nursing Administration*: January 2004 - Volume 34 - Issue 1 - pp 46-53.

Bekoff, Marc. *"Scientists Finally Conclude Nonhuman Animals Are Conscious Beings."* *Psychology Today.* Animal Emotions, 10 Aug. 2012.< https://www.psychologytoday.com/blog/animal-emotions/201208/scientists-finally-conclude-nonhuman-animals-are-conscious-beings>.

"The Biggest Comebacks of the Past 20 Years." *FastCompany.* April 2015.

Bossidy, Larry, Ram Charan, and Charles Burck. *Execution: The Discipline of Getting Things Done.* New York: Crown Business, 2002.

Boushey, H. and Glynn, S.J. "There Are Significant Business Costs to Replacing Employees." *American Progress.* November 16, 2012. <https://www.americanprogress.org/wp-content/uploads/2012/11/CostofTurnover.pdf>.

Bradford, Alfred S. *With Arrow, Sword, and Spear: A History of Warfare in the Ancient World*. Praeger Publishers. 2001

Bryson, John M., and William D. Roering. "Applying Private-Sector Strategic Planning in the Public Sector." *Journal of the American Planning Association* 53.1 (1987): 9-22.

Bullen, Christine V.; Rockart, John F. *A primer on critical success factors*. Center for Information Systems Research, Sloan School of Management. 1981

"The Cambridge Declaration on Consciousness." <http://fcmconference.org/img/CambridgeDeclarationOn-Consciousness.pdf>.

Campbell, B. *The Oxford Handbook of Warfare in the Classical World*. Oxford University Press, USA, 2013.

Canova D, Myers ML, Smith DE, et al. "Changing the future of tobacco marketing by understanding the mistakes of the past: lessons from "Lights". *Tobacco Control* 2001;10 (suppl I): i43–4.

Cardinal, Laura; Miller, Chet. "Strategic Planning and Firm Performance: A Synthesis of More Than Two Decades of Research." *Management Journal*. No.6, 1649-1665.

Cartwright, Mark. "Peloponnesian War." *Ancient History Encyclopedia*. Last modified June 01, 2013. <http://www.ancient.eu /Peloponnesian_War/>.

Centers for Disease Control and Prevention. "Current Cigarette Smoking Among Adults—United States, 2005–2012." *Morbidity and Mortality Weekly Report 2014*; 63(02):29–34

Chandler, Alfred D. *Chapters in the History of the American Industrial Enterprise*. Beard Books. 1962.

Christensen, Clayton M.; van Beverc, Derek; Wang, Dina. "Consulting on the Cusp of Disruption." *Harvard Business Review;* October 2013

Collis, David J., and Cynthia A. Montgomery. *Corporate Strategy: A Resource-based Approach*. Boston, MA: Irwin, McGraw-Hill, 1998.

Daiches, David. *Robert Burns*. New York: Macmillan, 1966

Daniel, D. Ronald. "Management Information Crisis." *Harvard Business Review*; September-October 1961, p. 111.

Davis, Alan M. 1993. *Software Requirements: Objects, Functions, and States*. Englewood Cliffs, NJ: Prentice-Hall.

Deming, W. Edwards. "Quality as a Business Strategy: Building a System of Improvement." *Associates in Process Improvement*. October 1999.

Deming, W. Edwards. *Quality, Productivity, and Competitive Position*. Cambridge, MA: Massachusetts Institute of Technology, Center for Advanced Engineering Study, 1982.

Dettmer, H. William., *The Logical Thinking Process: A Systems Approach to Complex Problem Solving*. Milwaukee, WI: ASQ Quality, 2007.

Dichter, Ernest. "Why Do We Smoke Cigarettes?" *The Psychology of Everyday Living*. 1947. <http://smokingsides.com/docs/whysmoke.html>.

Dinesh, David; Palmer, Elaine. "Management by objectives and the Balanced Scorecard: will Rome fall again?" *Management Decision*, Vol. 36 Iss: 6, pp.363 – 369. 1998.

Edwards, Tab. *I&O Strategy: Imaging & Output*. Oxford Hill Press, 2008.

"Employee Retention – How to Retain Employees." *The Wall Street Journal*. <http://guides.wsj.com/small-business/hiring-and-managing-employees/how-to-retain-employees/>.

Fisher, Christian. "The Average Employee Turnover in

Large Organizations." Demand Media. <http://work.chron.com/average-employee-turnover-large-organizations-29521.html>.

Friedrich, Bruce. "Chickens: smarter than a four-year-old." *New York Daily News*; August 16, 2013.

Fromson, By Brett D. "Slugfest in the Smoke Ring" *Washington Post*; Sunday, March 1, 1998; Page H01; <http://www.washingtonpost.com/wp-srv/national/longterm/tobacco/stories/slugfest.htm>.

Gause, G. F. "The Struggle for Existence." *Soil Science* 41.2 (1936): 159.

Gavetti, Giovanni, and Rivkin, Jan W. "On the Origin of Strategy: Action and Cognition over Time." *Organization Science*, Vol. 18, No. 3, May–June 2007, pp. 420–439

Goldratt, Eliyahu M., and Jeff Cox. *The Goal: A Process of Ongoing Improvement*. Great Barrington, MA: North River, 1992.

Greenwood, Ronald G. "Management by Objectives: As Developed by Peter Drucker, Assisted by Harold Smiddy." *The Academy of Management Review* 6.2 (1981): 225.

Gross, Daniel. *Forbes greatest business stories of all time*. J. Wiley & Sons, Oct 24, 1996

Growing Your Business: Strategies That Work for Small and Midsize Companies. Boston: Harvard Business School Pub., 2006.

Hardin, G. "The Competitive Exclusion Principle." *Science* 131.3409 (1960): 1292-297.

Hayman, J. and Mason, B. *Managing Employee Involvement and Participation*. London: Sage

Publications. 1995Henderson, Bruce. "The origin of Strategy: What Business Owes Darwin and other Reflections." *Harvard Business Review*. November-December 1989

Hindle, Tim. *Guide to Management Ideas and Gurus.* London: Profile, 2008.

Homkes, Rebecca; Sull, Donald; and Sull, Charles. "Why Strategy Execution Unravels—and What to Do About It." Harvard Business Review. March 2015.

"In U.S., Employment Most Linked to Being Depression-Free." Gallup, Inc. http://www.gallup.com/poll/164090/employment-linked-depression-free.aspx

Johnson, R., and Lubin, G. "The Smartest Computers in the World." *Business Insider.* 2011. <http://www.businessinsider.com/the-smartest-computers-in-the-world-2011-9>.

"Jump up!" R.J. Reynolds Marketing Report. October 6, 1989. 110 pp. at p. 39-40

Kay, Gannett Andrea. "At Work: Job, Self-esteem Tied Tightly Together. "*USA Today.* Gannett, 31 Aug. 2013.

Kozlowski LT, O'Connor RJ. "Cigarette filter ventilation is a defective design because of misleading taste, bigger puffs, and blocked vents." *Tobacco Control* 2002;11(suppl I):i40–50.

Langley GJ., Nolan KM., Norman CL., Provost LP. & Nolan TW. (1996).*The Improvement Guide: A Practical Approach to Enhancing Organizational Performance,* San Francisco: Jossey-Bass Publishers.

"Legacy Tobacco Documents Library : Competitive Strategic Assessment Updates... (lrz50f00)." *Legacy Tobacco Documents Library : Competitive Strategic Assessment Updates... (lrz50f00).* Brown & Williamson, 23 Nov. 1998.

Liddell-Hart, B. H. *Strategy* (2nd Edition). Frederick Praeger. 1967

"Lotka-Volterra Two Species Model." *Lotka-Volterra Predator-Prey Model.* http://www.stolaf.edu/people/mckelvey/envision.dir/lotka-volt.html

Mankins, Michael C., and Steele, Richard. "Turning

Great Strategy into Great Performance" Harvard Business Review. July 2005.

Marx, Karl, *Capital, A Critique of Political Economy (Das Kapital),* by Karl Marx. Frederick Engels, Ernest Untermann, eds. Samuel Moore, Edward Aveling, trans. 1906. Library of Economics and Liberty. 25 March 2015. <http://www.econlib.org/library/YPDBooks/ Marx/mrxCpContents.html>.

Maslow, A. H. «A Theory of Human Motivation.» *Psychological Review* 50.4 (1943): 370-96.

Merhar, Christina. «Employee Retention - The Real Cost of Losing an Employee.» *Employee Retention - The Real Cost of Losing an Employee.* Zane Benefits, Aug. 2013. <http://www.zanebenefits.com/blog/bid/312123/ Employee-Retention-The-Real-Cost-of-Losing-an-Employee>.

Michael, Allen; Shaked, Israel. "RJR Nabisco: A Case Study of a Complex Leveraged Buyout." *Financial Analysts Journal;* Sep/Oct 1991.

Microsoft Partner Network. <https://mspartner.microsoft. com/en/hk/Pages/Membership/core-benefits.aspx>

Mountain, Michael. "Scientists Declare: Nonhuman Animals Are Conscious." *Earth in Transition.* N.p., July-Aug. 2012.< http://www.earthintransition. org/2012/07/scientists-declare-nonhuman-animals-are-conscious/>.

O'Brien, Peggy, Jeanne Addison. Roberts, Michael Tolaydo, and Nancy Goodwin. *Shakespeare Set Free: Teaching Twelfth Night, Othello.* New York: Washington Square, 1995.

Ottinger, Randy. "Failed Strategy Execution Due to Oversight by Corporate Boards?" *Forbes.* 21 Oct. 2012.

"Peloponnesian War." *Ancient History Encyclopedia.*

Plutarch. *The Rise and Fall of Athens.* Penguin Classics, 1960.

Pollay, RW. "Filters, flavor . . . flim-flam, too!: cigarette advertising content and its regulation." *Journal of Public Policy and Marketing* 1989;8:30–9.

Pollay, RW, Dewhirst, T. "The dark side of marketing seemingly 'Light' cigarettes: successful images and failed fact." *Tobacco Control* 2002;11 (suppl I):i18–31.

Pollay, RW." Zebras in Russia! Where next?" *Tobacco Control* 2003; 12:89–90.

Porter, M. E. *Competitive Advantage: Creating and Sustaining Superior Performance.* Free Press, New York. 1985.

"Reynolds Tobacco Plans Cuts In U.S. Work Force." Chicago Tribune; June 04, 1987 | By United Press International.

Ries, Al, and Jack Trout. *The 22 Immutable Laws of Marketing.* London: Profile Business, 1994.

Rockart, John F. "Chief Executives Define Their Own Data Needs." *Harvard Business Review;* March-April 1979, p. 81.

Roisman, Joseph. *Ancient Greece from Homer to Alexander: The Evidence.* Chichester, West Sussex: Wiley-Blackwell, 2011.

Rudd, David. "Low smoke Cigarette Snuffed Out After Tests." *Chicago Tribune;* March 01, 1989

Rudd, David C. "Reynolds Hopes Less Smoke Means More Cigarette Sales." *Chicago Tribune;* September 15, 1988

Silos, I.M. "Employee involvement – a component of total quality management." *Production & Inventory Management Journal,* Vol. 40, No. 1, pp. 56-65. 1999.

Spender, John-Christopher. "What do Managers Really do for their Organizations?" *European Management Journal;* Volume 7 No. 10. 1989.

Strassler, Robert B; Thucydides. *The Landmark Thucydides: A Comprehensive Guide to the Peloponnesian War;* Paperback – September 10, 1998

Steinberg, Neil. *Complete & Utter Failure: A Celebration of Also-rans, Runners-up, Never-weres, and Total Flops.* New York: Doubleday, 1994.

"Three Reasons Why Good Strategies Fail: Execution, Execution…." *Knowledge@Wharton.* The Wharton School, University of Pennsylvania, 10 August, 2005. Web. 06 April, 2015 <http://knowledge.wharton.upenn.edu/article/three-reasons-why-good-strategies-fail-execution-execution/>

«Tobacco and Health.» *Tobacco & Health.* Maine Department of Health and Human Services. http://www.tobaccofreemaine.org/explore_facts/tobacco_and_health.php

"Tobacco Use: United States, 1900-1999." *Oncology;* November 30, 1999.

"Trends in Current Cigarette Smoking Among High School Students and Adults, United States, 1965–2011." *Centers for Disease Control and Prevention.* Centers for Disease Control and Prevention, 14 Nov. 2013.

Warry, John. "Peloponnesian War." Warfare in the Classical World, 1995. *Http://www.laconia.org/gen_info_literature/Peloponnesian_war.htm.*

"Why did the chicken cross the road?" *The Knickerbocker,* or *The New York Monthly*, March 1847, p. 283. Wikipedia. http://en.wikipedia.org/wiki/Why_did_the_chicken_cross_the_road%3F#cite_ref-1

INDEX